HOW TO GET OUT

:::::::::::::::::::::::::::::::: *of the* ::::::::::::::::::::::::::::::::

FRIEND ZONE

HOW TO GET OUT

:::::::::::::::::::::::::::::::::::: *of the* ::::::::::::::::::::::::::::::::::::

FRIEND ZONE

TURN YOUR *friendship*
INTO A *relationship*

The Wing Girls
JET & STAR

CHRONICLE BOOKS
SAN FRANCISCO

Library of Congress Cataloging-in-Publication Data:

Russo, Miranda.

  How to get out of the friend zone : turn your friendship into a relationship / The Wing girls, Miranda Russo, Tracy Wilcoxen.

     pages cm

  ISBN 978-1-4521-0918-3

1. Dating—Humor. 2. Man-Woman relationships Humor. I. Wilcoxen, Tracy II. Title.

  PN6231.D3R68 2013

  818'.602—dc23

                          2013001833

Manufactured in China

Design and typesetting by NOON SF

Typeset in Archer and DIN

The Wing Girls™ is a registered trademark of Miranda Russo and Tracy Wilcoxen.

10 9 8 7 6 5 4 3 2 1

Chronicle Books LLC

680 Second Street

San Francisco, California 94107

www.chroniclebooks.com

TO RAFFI

···

a girl after our own heart,
who will most definitely run
the world one day

Contents

· ·

Part One: WHAT IS THE FRIEND ZONE AND ARE YOU IN IT?

· ·

Part Two: GETTING OUT

Acknowledgments

This book came about when an eighth-grader named Raffi watched our YouTube video "Why Geeks Make Better Boyfriends" and then convinced her mother, literary agent Betsy Lerner, that we should write a book. Without her, *How To Get Out of The Friend Zone* would never have come to be.

We are beyond grateful for Betsy, who always kept it real, believed in us when others didn't, and taught us to never count our chickens until we were eating egg salad sandwiches. She made us part of her family, even when we ordered way too many things at the Chateau Marmont.

We are forever indebted to our editor, Leigh Haber, for never holding back her honest opinion and always pushing us to go further. Plus, without her, this book would have more profanity than a f&*@in' roomful of sailors.

Our heartfelt gratitude goes out to Lorena Jones, Elizabeth Yarborough, and everyone at Chronicle Books. We needed the one "yes," and they gave us that. A few months ago, we were walking home after a day full of editing when a man came up to us with three plastic bags full of paperbacks. He said he was selling his self-published book and asked if we would buy a copy. The price was twenty dollars, so we paid twelve and walked away, thanking our lucky stars we had a publisher.

Special thanks to Ashley, John, Yessie, Ian, Julie, Joanna, and Mike T. for sharing their stories and filling out our boring questionnaire. And thank you to Allen Zadoff for meeting with us and telling us it was okay to be baby writers.

To every guy who put us in the Friend Zone: Devan, Domenic, Jake, Tim, Drew, and those who shall remain nameless: we love you, we hate you, we love you.

To everyone we put in the Friend Zone: Alex, Elan, Fred, Jeff, Dave, Vincent, Bob, and probably a bunch of other people we didn't even know about: sorry, we suck.

And last but *definitely* not least, a very special thanks to all our Wing Girls fans. Thanks to all of them for watching our show, supporting us, encouraging us, and, most important, for buying this book.

FROM STAR

I could never have written this book without my parents, because without them, I wouldn't have been born. For all the love, support, and encouragement they provide each and every day, I could not be luckier, and I know it. I also have to thank my sister, Lisa, who is my therapist, my voice of reason, and my favorite person to laugh with. Special thanks to my LP, Andrew, who puts up with all my crazy ideas and inspires many more. My high school self could not be any more thrilled with the way it all worked out. Special love and thanks to all my friends, for their words of encouragement, support, and for buying me drinks after long days in front of the computer.

FROM JET

To my family, who asked if anyone wanted more artichoke dip when I announced my book deal. Thanks to all of them for their love and undying support of this book and all my other creative endeavors, including but not limited to my three-strum guitar lessons, my photography and subsequent darkroom creation that never quite took off, the play I started writing and never finished, and the front-porch production of *The Wizard of Oz*, where I forced my brother to wear a dress and ride an exercise bike. Thanks to Al, who laughs out loud at literally everything I write or do, for believing in me 100 percent. To my parents for supporting me in every way I could possibly ask for: from paying for my car insurance to pushing me to pursue my dreams. I know that no matter what I do, they will always treat me like a star. Also, thanks to my friends for all their support and encouragement. And a special thanks to everyone who mentioned their own bestselling book ideas the second they learned about our book deal.

THE FRIEND ZONE
(noun)

1. The condition of being in love with someone who only sees you as a shoulder to cry on; a wrestling partner; a midnight airport picker-upper; and a general, platonic, kiss-you-on-the-forehead grade-A friend

Introduction

The defining feature of any Friend Zone relationship is the ambiguity. The not knowing where you stand, the blurred boundaries, the vague flirtations. It's all so tear-your-hair-out confusing. Think about it. No other state of friendship or relationship has its own zone. There's no "engagement zone" or "getting to know a new coworker zone." That's because most stages in a relationship are temporary. The Friend Zone is an endless wasteland of frustration, sadness, sexual tension, desperation, and longing—with little oases of hope sprinkled in to keep you there. Some people only stay for a few months, others take up permanent residency. No matter how long you've already been there, this book will help you get out and stay out, once and for all. Because you deserve better than spending the rest of your days fantasizing about a relationship, when you should be having one.

OUR STORIES

No one wants to hear about the Friend Zone from someone who hasn't been in the thick of it. That's like getting flying lessons from a person who's never even been in a plane. Lucky for you, we've been there—on both sides. We've stayed up nights devising plans for our escape and made others wonder if they were ever getting out. Read on for our own tales of Friend Zone woe.

Star & the Friend Zone

I've had many Friend Zone experiences throughout my life, but my first and most defining Friend Zone relationship was in high school. His name was Daniel Becker. To anyone else, he may have just seemed like your average run-of-the-mill band geek, but to me, he was *it*: the be-all, end-all of the universe, thank you and good night. He was my everything, and we were going to get married, have at least two babies, and live happily ever after one block from Disneyland, where we would sing "love songs after dark" to each other every night. But the fact was, he barely knew me. The closest contact we'd actually had was in middle school, in chorus, when I played a yellow crayon and he an orange one. That didn't matter to me, though, because I was going to make him love me. I had always gotten the things I wanted by being incredibly persistent, like becoming co-captain of the drill team and treasurer of the Spanish club, so why wouldn't the same tactic work when it came to Daniel? I would just wear him down until he finally realized he couldn't live without me.

I memorized his schedule and just "happened" to be outside the music room when band practice ended. I dropped by his house to bring him butter pecan ice cream, because I knew that was his favorite. I even switched into physics so that we would be in the same class. I figured that all he had to do was get to know me and then we would fall madly in love and he'd kiss me on the football bleachers in front of all his friends. It never occurred to my dense high school brain that while this method was fine for club leadership roles, it might not work for attracting boyfriends.

All that effort paid off in a way, but not exactly how I hoped. We became really close "friends." We started hanging out together all the time—going to the mall, bowling, singing karaoke together. We had a grand old time. We laughed so hard our cheeks hurt and spent the whole weekend talking on the phone. Oh, yeah, we wrestled and tickled and gave each other back massages, too. If anyone was watching us, they would think we were the cutest lovebirds you ever saw. We were sooooo in love. Except *we* weren't. While I was head-over-heels-I-can't-even-breathe-when-he's-around in *looooove*, he thought of me merely as a good friend, a buddy, a little sister. And unbeknownst to me, he didn't see me as anything more than that.

One night, as I drove us home from ice-skating, I decided to finally make my move. My palms were sweating. I felt like I was going to throw up. But I had to go through with it, so I turned to Daniel and asked him, "Have you ever thought about us dating?" He immediately looked really uncomfortable, but then he said, "Yeah, I've thought about it." I moved closer to him. This was the moment I'd been waiting for. Until the "but." "But our friendship is really important to me," he continued, "and I wouldn't want to ruin it by dating." I was crushed. I felt my heart drop out of my chest. I couldn't look at him out of fear that I would burst into tears. Here I'd been spending all this time and effort, plotting, planning, and calculating my way into becoming his friend so he'd see how fun and smart I was and then fall madly in love with me. But I'd done such a good job of pretending to be his friend that he couldn't see me as anything else. Soon after that, he started dating a girl who was the polar opposite of me. She was always coy and distant and pretended she barely knew Daniel's name. They even ended up going to prom together, while I stayed home watching *The Notebook* for the ninetieth time and wondering why I was alone on the couch while she was twirling around in a sparkly dress.

Thus concluded my first and most painful experience with the Friend Zone. You never forget your first time, right? While I left this relationship behind when high school ended, the scars that I earned from it stayed with me long after.

In my twenties, probably because I had done more than my fair share of time in the Friend Zone, and because karma's a bitch, I relegated a few guy friends of my own to the Friend Zone. The truth is, I would have been lucky to date any of them. They were all smart, funny, accomplished, successful—all-around great guys. I look back now and I want to kick myself for treating them the way I did. But I also wish someone could have gotten to them first and told them what they were doing wrong. Andre was too available. If I said "Jump," he'd go buy a trampoline. It was so obvious to me that he liked me, and honestly, I like the chase. The chase is fun. If only he had waited a day to call me back, just once. Evan, on the other hand, was cool in an "I've been all over the world three times" kind of way. I'd never met anyone like him. He knew about everything: communist Russia, medieval poetry, white rappers. He was smart. But he had bad teeth and chronically chapped lips, which I couldn't imagine kissing. I worried chapped lips were contagious. Couldn't someone tell him to exfoliate those babies?

Then there was Jeremy. He became my therapist during a period when I was acting as a regular motel for jerky guys. Jeremy would just sit there and listen to me talk about all my problems, offer advice, and hold me while I cried. When he finally told me he wanted to date me, I had already stopped going to my regular therapist, because I had Jeremy now. And I couldn't date him, because wouldn't that violate the doctor-patient relationship? Plus, he knew how crazy I was, so how could I be his girlfriend? Didn't he know that letting a girl sob on his shoulder would never get him into her pants?

Clearly my own hang-ups were partly to blame for my failure to recognize these guys' romantic potential, but then again, they could have taken some actions to turn the odds in their favor. If this book had been around back then, things might have turned out a lot differently.

Jet & the Friend Zone

I spent most of high school having over-the-top crushes on guys who would have referred to me as a "really good friend." Their amigo. Their buddy. One of the guys. But for me, it was true love, and our "friendships" were just an excuse to do creepy stalker things that at the time seemed totally normal to me, like changing seating charts so I could sit next to them in class, repeatedly driving by their house with no intention of actually stopping, taking pictures with them to put in my journal, and sometimes even sleeping next to them in their bed when they were passed out. I would hang out with them until the wee hours of the morning, watching them party until they inevitably hooked up with one of my many skinny blonde friends.

I told myself that one day they would stop being afraid or intimidated by my booming voice and crass sense of humor and would come around to falling in love with me, confessing it to the whole school and maybe fighting over me with other popular guys. This is the story I would tell myself while bingeing on cold canned ravioli after a long night of giving them back massages. One day they'd get it.

My seduction strategy was to hang out with them long enough to wear them down, kind of like a police interrogation. I reasoned that eventually they'd crack under pressure. One night they'd just snap, sweep me off my feet, take away my virginity, and dedicate their band's next song to me.

At times they *did* give me mixed messages, like telling a mutual friend that I was "really beautiful" or holding my hand in public. But the reality was, these people were so far out of my league it was ridiculous. I aimed high. Hottest-guy-in-school high. Cheerleader-girlfriend high. True, on the inside I was a better person than all of them put together. And I was very good socially, I had a ton of friends; some might have even called me popular. But I couldn't dress or do my hair to save my life. I didn't outfit myself like the pretty popular girls, and I hid my enormous boobs, which could have been a major selling point, under loose, extremely unflattering clothing, because I was so deathly ashamed of them. Who knew corduroy old-man pants and a Mickey Mouse sweatshirt weren't sexy?

Sexy scared the living daylights out of me. I thought that boobs and a sexy body would separate me from being one of the guys, and that would spoil my plans of winning them over without them noticing, without them treating me differently. Besides, popular guys in high school didn't like girls like me anyway. I was too loud, and way too out there.

So how did they feel about me? If I were to really look at my many Friend Zone situations with all honesty, they all saw me as a loud, chubby, funny, neurotic, annoying girl/boy. It was too much for a high school Adonis to take on. Don't get me wrong, I had a few boyfriends, but they weren't the ones I was stalking. They were the smart, kind ones that I was ignoring. And the guys I really liked didn't return my feelings for them. Maybe a part of them, for a short minute or two, had some affection for me, but I'm sure I burped or fell down a flight of stairs before they could give it a second thought. I was shooting myself in my own worn-out high-tops and making sure no one who I liked could like me in any real way.

As the true Friend Zone survivor that I am, after high school, I threw a few dozen guys into the Zone myself. I would go to college parties and hang all over guys and be genuinely shocked when they asked me on dates or confessed their love to me. I was taken completely off guard. I would literally lie on top of guys and be weirded out when they had erections. I guess I had spent so much time in the Friend Zone, I thought that's how you treated a friend. I never thought anyone liked me, because I had spent so many years pining after guys who never would. It's a vicious cycle. Years later, when I finally realized that I was doing to other people the very same thing that hurt me the most, I stopped. I remember telling a guy he reminded me of my brother, after I had spent the whole night cuddled up against him. His face dropped in such a heartbreakingly familiar way that I just couldn't help but make the connection. I was the high school Adonis and he the chubby, strange girl.

WHY WE WROTE THIS BOOK

At first we thought our experiences were unique. We stamped these tragic stories with the label of "unrequited love" and filed them away, never to think of them again, until . . . we met. We had each just moved to Los Angeles to work in comedy. One night we were both dragged to the same party at a hipster's house in the Hollywood Hills. Out by the infinity pool, a very intoxicated guy was loudly complaining about not getting a date. We both started doling out advice, and by the end of the night, we had forgotten all about him and a friendship was born.

At first, we were just venting to each other about our frustrations with dating. We would stay up until 2 A.M. saying things like, "I wish every guy just knew . . ." or "If only someone would tell these dudes exactly what to do!" Then it became: "Why don't we just tell them?" And so we started our blog to divulge the ugly truth to guys everywhere, the secrets that girls wouldn't tell them face-to-face. We didn't know them personally, so we had nothing to lose. They were relatively simple directions: "Don't leave right after you hook up with a girl" or "Call her the next day—the three-day rule is so over." We adopted a tough-love approach, saying what guys needed to hear, but in a funny way so they actually listened. We weren't sugarcoating anything, and that really resonated with our readers.

Then we realized we could help even more people if we started making videos. From this idea, the Web series "The Wing Girls" was born. In each video, we took a topic, like How to Tell if She Likes You or What Not to Say on a First Date, and gave our take on it: a mix of comedy, uncomfortable truths, and helpful information. To our surprise and amazement, the videos caught on and we developed a loyal fan base from all over the world.

In the seven years since we created "The Wing Girls," our videos have racked up more than one hundred million views. Many of these viewers wrote to us personally and asked for help in their dating lives. We got messages from people all over the world, people of all ages. Out of all of these letters, one theme kept showing up over and over again. There was that familiar, desperate hopelessness that only a person who has been there before could recognize. It struck us to the core. Each of these messages had the same story: someone waiting in the wings for their friend to recognize how perfect they would be together. "If I wait long enough, he'll realize that I'm the one for him." Or "If I'm there for her every time she cries, eventually she'll see that I'm her knight in shining armor." It was like getting a bunch of letters from prison inmates, only their imprisonment was self-assigned.

We talked about it at length, trying to figure out why we were hearing the same story over and over again. There was a guy in Ireland with the exact same problem as a girl in Fort Worth, Texas. Yes, we heard about breakups, and being too shy to ask someone out, but the most frequent and desperate pleas came from people sharing one common problem.

Not only did it take up most of our day to respond to each of these lovelorn people, but it also gave us PTSD flashbacks to our own battles. Why did all these letters bring up such familiar feelings for us? We knew firsthand the pain that these people spoke of. Everyone was trapped in the same conundrum: "I'm in love with my friend, and they don't see me as anything more than that." That's when it hit us. This wasn't case after case of unrequited love. This was *the Friend Zone.*

We were in an extraordinarily excellent position to see it all: the patterns, the similarities, what worked, what didn't. We were on the front lines of the Friend Zone battlefield, privy to the internal war that people were fighting against themselves in the name of love. We read so many letters, met with so many people, gave out so much advice about the Friend Zone that now we can spot a Friend Zone situation from a mile away. We can walk through a café and point out which couples are stuck in the Friend Zone and which will be going home later to get it on. Our special area of expertise isn't something we studied for. We don't have PhDs in Friend Zoneology, but we've done plenty of work in the field. Everything we know, we learned through experience.

Since we were hearing from people on either side of the Friend Zone fence—those in it, and those putting others there—we could see what each party needed to do to succeed. We combined our personal experiences with the hundreds of cases from the people who wrote to us and came up with a step-by-step program to get out of the Friend Zone. It started out as a theory but needed to be put to the test. Right around that time, one of our fans came to us and asked for help with his Friend Zone situation. He was friends with a girl in his dorm, and she was giving him a ton of mixed

Dear Wing Girls:

I feel like I was put in the Friend Zone. Our conversations are always sarcastic flirting-type convos but she said she liked me as a friend and thinks I'm funny. I asked her out over iChat last week and she said "LOL." What's up?

Hi WG:

I met this guy when I was going to college. At the time he was on and off with his ex. He invited me out for ice cream and we had the best time together. I totally thought he was going to ask me to be his girlfriend. Since then (four years ago) we've gone to the movies a few times, had lunch/dinner etc. and text all the time. But he's back with his ex and he's never made a move on me. I know he likes me, but I'm getting kind of impatient. Am I stupid to wait around for him?

Hey WG:

Well, I've been hanging out with this girl for a month. We have been co-workers for two years now but recently started going out on "dates." However, whenever I go in for a kiss, she gives me the cheek. Why does she do that?

Hi Jet, Hi Star:

There's this girl, who's my friend. She said she doesn't like me like that but she knows I have a crush on her, I told her. She ignored me for about a month. Now she started talking to me again. What ulterior motive would she have in calling me? Should I start hitting on her again? Does this mean nothing?

messages. She'd spend the night in his room and the next day ask him for love advice about the jock across the hall. He really liked her, but he was out of ideas. We told him we were coming up with a system and asked if he would try it out for us. He happily agreed. We told him exactly what to do. He followed our advice to a T and was shocked when our theory actually worked. His "friend" became his girlfriend, and he was forever indebted to us. Since it worked for him, we were hopeful, but we weren't popping out the champagne yet. We rounded up some other people who were stuck in the Friend Zone and had them try it too. When it worked for them, we knew we were on to something big.

With so many success stories on our hands, we decided to put our system down on paper so that no one would ever have to live through another one of those cringe-inducing "I only see you as a friend" conversations again. It wasn't fair to keep the solution to ourselves. That would be like sitting on a gold mine and watching the jewelry store across the street go out of business.

This book is for anyone who's tired of spending night after night pining over someone who only sees them as a ride to work. This is for anyone who continually puts people in the Friend Zone, whether consciously or not, and who finds that it has finally come around to bite them on the backside. It's for those who might not currently be in the Friend Zone but have spent a lot of time in that zip code and want to break the pattern once and for all. In other words, this book is for you.

"THANK YOU! THANK YOU! THANK YOU! THIS WAS LIFE-CHANGING!"

"Amazing! I finally got out of the Friend Zone with a man I followed around like a dog for years!"

"This actually worked. I can't believe it! I'm dating him now. I have to pinch myself all the time. I owe you ladies."

"WOW, IT REALLY WORKED. I GOT A GIRLFRIEND, AND THE GIRL I LIKED BEFORE LIKES ME NOW TOO. I'M SHOCKED!"

"I HAD NO IDEA I WAS DOING EVERYTHING WRONG, FOR SO LONG. THANK YOU FOR MAKING ME SEE THE LIGHT. I'LL NEVER GO BACK TO THE FRIEND ZONE AGAIN."

"I just wanted to thank you for the advice. Because of you I got out of the Friend Zone and now I've been with my boyfriend for two and a half years."

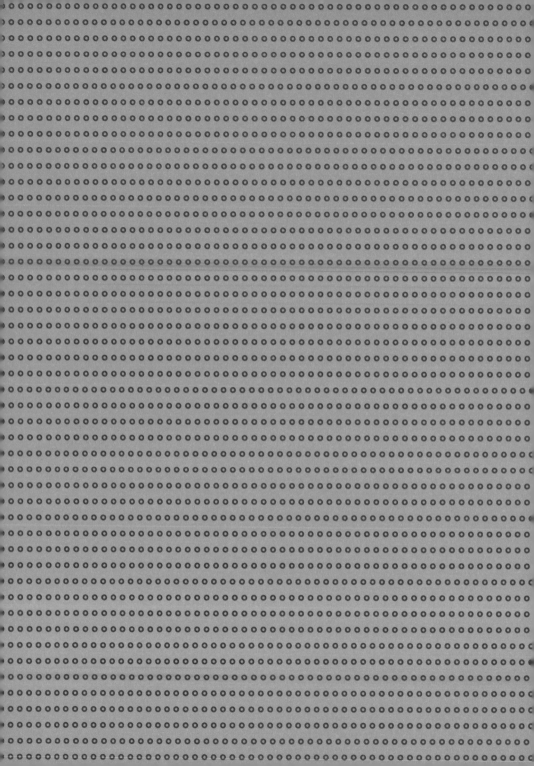

Part One

· ·

WHAT IS THE FRIEND ZONE AND ARE YOU IN IT?

CHAPTER 1

The Truth About the Friend Zone

What you're doing isn't working. There, we said it. The thing your friends, family, and, yes, even crazy Linda from the Coffee Bean are thinking. You know that "special person" you think about every night as you fall asleep, a.k.a. your friend? You think that if you answer the phone on the first ring every time your friend calls, and free up your weekends just in case they need someone to help them move, eventually your friend will come to their senses and realize they absolutely have to sleep with you, not only today, but for the rest of their God-given lives. We're not talking about just sex, we're talking about *loooove*-making, the kind where you gaze into each other's eyes, weep tears of joy, and shoot rainbows into each others' hearts. We are talking about babies, and white picket fences, and home for the holidays. The real deal.

But here's the problem: everything you're currently doing is taking you further away from transforming this fantasy into reality. Your instincts are wrong, your gut feeling is wrong, your intuition is wrong. If this weren't the case, you and your friend would already be together. It's time to take a different approach. Take everything you think you know and chuck it. Now you are a blank slate. You are the hottest blank slate to ever walk the earth.

WHAT IS THE FRIEND ZONE?

The Friend Zone is the cold-and-lonely-getting-nowhere-fast dead end that is every beating heart's worst nightmare. You might think this sounds a bit dramatic, but so does platonically spooning someone you've been in love with for five years. You know what we're talking about or else you wouldn't have picked up this book, or bought it online in a cold sweat at 3 A.M. But for those of you who need a little clarification, the Friend Zone is when you're stuck in a "friendship" that you wish were a real lovey-dovey relationship. You hang out with this person, you fantasize about this person, but when somebody asks them who you are, they say, "Oh, that's my friend." It's like a dagger to the heart. You cling to the hope that if your friend just knew how you felt inside, or if they saw you as the great catch that you are, that they would throw their arms around you and you would drive off together on a motorcycle into the sunset. Unfortunately, that day rarely comes.

The sad truth is that most people who are stuck deep in the Friend Zone have absolutely no idea they are in it, or want so badly to not be in it that they convince themselves they're not. Everyone thinks they're the exception to the rule. "I'm totally not in the Friend Zone. We just have a really complicated situation." Yes, everyone's different. Yes, we are all unique, special little snowflakes. But there are certain patterns that come up in every Friend Zone relationship, and we're going to tell you what they are.

HERE'S WHAT IT LOOKS LIKE

From the outside, a Friend Zone relationship looks almost exactly like a real relationship. You two are inseparable. You go shopping together, you instant message constantly, you go to dinner at the same pizza place every Thursday and play thumb war to decide who gets to choose the toppings, you go on road trips and sing old Disney songs, you go to Ikea and sit in the showroom and pretend you live together and fight over the fake remote. You are the cutest damn couple this world has ever seen. You're so cute, it makes old people smile when they look at you. You're just cute, cute, cute, cute, cute! Only you're not a real couple. You're a couple whose relationship is as fake as that Ikea remote.

After a whole day spent with your friend, you hate yourself because you know you're lying. Here you are pretending to be someone's bestie when what you really want to do is make them your lovah. You spend the whole time you're with your friend thinking about how to make them more than your friend, and when you're not with them all you do is think about the next time you're going to be with them and what you're going to do differently. But then there you go again, doing the same thing day after day and wishing for a different ending. You feel kind of addicted to your friend, like the way you're addicted to curly fries, or to checking Facebook. You just can't get enough of the way you feel when you're with them, giddy, silly, like you're walking on air. You tell yourself you can stop anytime you want to. But when your friend calls out of the blue to see if you can go yard saling with them, the thought of saying no makes a little part of your heart die. You want them to love you so badly that it's hard to breathe. Your life is a roller coaster of highs and lows. Sometimes you look into your friend's eyes and couldn't be happier. Everything is perfect and you're exactly where you want to be. Other times it physically hurts to be with them because you're reminded of how perfect your life would be if only they were yours.

Your buddies all think you guys are in love and tease you about how you're already married to your friend, and that's why you never have a date. You always shrug them off and tell them that you are totally open to dating, that the right person hasn't come along yet so you're keeping your options open, but secretly you know that it would take a supermodel/Nobel Prize winner to pry your heart away from your friend's grasp. You tell yourself that if you could just get up the guts to confess your feelings to your friend, you two would live happily ever after in a castle, or at least a nice two-story Craftsman. Sometimes you think that if you just changed one little part of yourself, like if you lost ten pounds, or found the right haircut, or got that teeth whitening laser stuff, or became a rock star, that they would suddenly run to you in slow motion, like in all those romantic comedies, and throw their arms around you and say, "What have we been waiting for?" At the same time, you have a recurring nightmare that they get married to the wrong person (as in anyone who's not you). If that really happened, you'd have to move to Iceland and become a trapeze artist or a shrimp boat captain. You are always walking that tight-rope between best- and worst-case scenarios.

WHY IS IT A PROBLEM?

Some of you may be asking, "Why is it a problem? I'm happy here whistling in the dark. I love my fake relationship where I feel super-bad about myself and don't get laid! It's fun to be tortured on a regular basis. Snuggling with my body pillow is enough for me." Is it really? Look at your Friend Zone situation for what it really is:

It's a relationship built on a deck of cards. At any moment your whole world could be turned upside down because your friend fell for someone else. You think, "If they would just stay exactly where they are, paralyzed in time for the rest of eternity, I would be happy, but if they move slightly to the right or left, it would all go to hell." This is a conditional relationship where you have no say over what happens to you. You have no control over your own fate.

Also, you're not getting laid by the person you want to get laid by. What are you? A nun? Why on earth would you do this to yourself? "A self-imposed abstinence? Sure, sign me up!" Do you not like sex? Are you sure? It feels pretty good. And no matter what anyone says, it does wonders for your self-esteem to be with someone, in an intimate way, who you are physically attracted to, and you deserve that.

You're doing all the hard work for no reward. You're doing the homework and someone else is getting the A. Maybe you're pump-ing up their ego so they can have the courage to date someone else. Maybe you're giving them free therapy or helping them break out of their shell. Whatever it is, you're doing it for your friend and not for yourself. You are essentially picking up someone else's dog poop off someone else's lawn. You should only do that for your own dog. Why are you putting in all this emotional time and effort and getting nothing in return?

You are also lying. Not admitting your true feelings for your friend is lying. If your friend knew about your true feelings for them, it would change the dynamic of your relationship. You know this, but you're keeping it to yourself because you're afraid. If you were withholding any other information this important, you wouldn't be able to sleep at night, but since it's just the fact that you're in love, you feel you can let it slide.

You're getting in your own way. The world is full of people who will hinder your future relationships; you don't need to be one of them. The fantasy of being with your friend is preventing you from entering a real relationship. Even though you say you're open to dating other people and finding someone else, be honest. You're not really looking, because you've got your heart set on this friend of yours.

Your other friends feel sorry for you and are tired of hearing the same thing over and over again. They cringe when you talk about your friend. You're the friend who needs an intervention. They shake their heads and mouth the words "Friend Zone" to each other every time you mention your friend's name. They feel powerless to help you because you ignore everything they suggest. They know you're in a terrible situation, but they don't know what to do about it, so they just sit on the sidelines and pray that you'll meet someone else and move on with your life.

Also, you are undervaluing yourself. You should be with someone who can't believe they get to be with a person as cool as you, and you can't believe it either. And together you are amazed at how lucky you were to find each other. Why would you settle for less than that? And yes, being with someone who doesn't love you back is settling. You may think it's not because you are striving for someone who, in your mind, is the best thing on the planet. The truth is you're settling when you have anything less than an actual relationship, and P.S.: pining after someone you secretly love is not an actual relationship, no matter how much you pretend.

Last but not least, you're not getting any younger. Life is short, and here you are messing around in some vague situation with someone who may or may not like you in that way, while the rest of the world is in love and moving forward. By staying in this relationship for too long, you're keeping yourself from meeting someone else. Before you know it, you've spent your prime dating years treading water in some murky relationship, never knowing if you're going to make it out of the deep end. Quick, while you're still in your prime, make something happen!

WHY YOU WANT TO STAY

Part of you secretly wants to stay in the Friend Zone forever, because it's safe. It's easier to let your perfect fantasy relationship play out in your head, because as long as it stays in your head, it can stay perfect. You can't mess it up by saying the wrong thing or doing something stupid. You're used to pining for the one you love. In reality, you wouldn't know what to do with yourself if your friend walked right up to you and said, "Hey, let's make babies." You'd probably drop dead right there. Let's face it: the Friend Zone is comfortable. It's torturous, sure, but at least you know what to expect. On the other side is completely unknown territory. The part of you that doesn't think you deserve any better is the same part that wants you to stay where it's comfortable to avoid getting hurt. And that's the part of you that's going to shut up and take one for the team. Because no one has ever gotten anything good without doing something a little scary and a little uncomfortable.

THAT'S GREAT. NOW WHAT?

We hear that voice inside your head yelling, "There's no way out! I'm done for! My life is over!" Well, here's the amazing, wonderful, life-changing news: there is a way out. Trust us. We've had a ton of successes; you might as well be one of them. You're sexy, smart, funny, and an all-around amazing catch. *Now* is the time to make a change, a real life change. You don't want to be in the nursing home and know that you spent your whole life pining for someone who never saw you as anything but a shoulder to cry on. You don't want to spend years watching from the sidelines as your friend, the person you love more than anyone in the world, gets married to someone (who isn't you), has babies (who don't look like you), and then sends you a Christmas card every year that says "Seasons Greetings from our family to yours" (even though you don't have a family, unless you count your fifteen cats).

There is hope for you and your Friend Zone situation, and there's a plan, with actual steps. In the chapters ahead, we'll walk you out of that hot mess you're currently in and into a situation that's better for you (and your poor friends, who can't listen to your spiel one more time). Our goal is to hand you the solution on a silver platter. Whether or not you take it is up to you. You want to get out of the Friend Zone? We have the answer, so what are you waiting for? Let's do this!

✧✧✧✧✧✧✧✧

Dear Wing Girls:

I have been hanging out with this guy for a while now. We have so much fun together and have gotten really close. I thought we were dating over the past few months and getting to know each other. But the other day, he asked me for advice about another girl he likes. I was shocked. Why would he ask me about someone else? My sister said I'm in his Friend Zone. Is that what's really going on? How is it possible I thought we were dating when he thought we were just friends? I didn't even know girls could be put in the Friend Zone!

✧✧✧✧✧✧✧✧

CHAPTER 2

Different Types of Friend Zones

The Friend Zone comes in many different forms. You can be in the Friend Zone with a coworker, a classmate, or your bestie. You can even be in the Friend Zone with someone you don't hang out with that much. That's right: no friendship is immune. And the deeper in the Friend Zone quicksand you are, the harder it is to get out.

The Friend Zone is a forest, and you can't see it for the trees. Sometimes you need to see your scenario from a distance to recognize what's really going on. So to help you see the big picture, here are some examples of different types of Friend Zone relationships. Note: You can be in one type or a combination of several types of these Friend Zone relationships. Try to focus on where your situation is similar, not where it's different.

THE BFF FOR LIFE
When you're truly best friends with someone
you are secretly in love with.

John and Kelly have known each other for the past ten years. They talk online every night, sometimes for hours. He invites her hiking with him on Saturdays, and she always goes, even though she secretly hates hiking and is deathly afraid of mountain lions. He just brought her to his best friend's wedding, and they danced the night away to cheesy '80s music. They go on road trips together and play that game where they punch each other's arms until they're black-and-blue. They know all of each other's secrets, even ones that Kelly wishes she didn't know, like how John has sex dreams about Mila Kunis.

Kelly believes they are perfect for each other. When she listens to Adele songs, she often mouths the words with him in mind. Kelly waits for the day when John will finally kiss her, on the mouth. She has a box of keepsakes from their times together and hopes to show it to their children one day. (Their names will be Brandon and Abigail.) She uses his last name as her password. There's only one problem: John and Kelly are not boyfriend and girlfriend; they are best friends. She loves him but has never expressed her true feelings. She knows him so well and he relies on her so much that the idea of actually crossing the line seems next to impossible. Kelly is stuck in relationship purgatory, where even though she wants more, she's not willing to risk the friendship by going for it.

The BFF is basically a full-fledged relationship without the sex. You go shopping, make dinner, watch a movie, and maybe even cuddle. But then you go home to the loneliness of your Craigslist futon, or, even worse, stay on your BFF's fold-out couch. You are in a relationship that could completely change at any moment, depending on the other person's dating life. You get a lot out of this type of Friend Zone relationship, so much so that you're afraid to lose what you have for the possibility of what you really want.

Victor and Jessica met at Dartmouth freshman year. Jessica smiled at Victor in the library and asked him to be in her study group. She seemed really happy to learn they had two classes together. Then she asked him to go with her to a friend's Pimps and Hos party, which she later deemed sexist and gross, so they spent most of the night on the back porch making fun of everyone. Then she slyly worked her boyfriend into the conversation, saying he would love this party, and that he was at ASU living it up. For the last three years, Victor and Jessica have been joined at the hip. They go to the pub crawl every month, they study in each other's dorm rooms, they text constantly. When Jessica goes to visit her boyfriend in California, Victor drives her to the airport. When she's gone, he notices he doesn't have a lot of friends. He gets sad and it makes him sick that she's with some other guy. Victor loves Jessica and believes she loves him too. When his roommate asks why he hasn't ever made a move, he says he's waiting for Jessica to break up with her boyfriend before he takes that step. He thinks the more time he spends with her, the closer they'll get, and then she'll realize they need to be together. So he waits, and waits, and waits.

In this scenario, someone else has already taken the object of your affection. From what we've seen in our dealings with the Friend Zone, the person that your friend is dating is most likely the exact opposite of you, hence your friend's need to have you in their life. If you are shy, their boyfriend or girlfriend is most likely outgoing, or if you pay for everything, their significant other is probably a cheapo. You are providing what your friend isn't getting from the other person. You are filling that void. Lucky you, the sexless void-filler. Look, if the person your friend is with were just like you, there would be no need for you. They don't have to choose between the two of you because they get to keep you both.

> ### THE USE
> *An extremely one-sided friendship where you will say and do anything to make your friend happy. You allow yourself to be used in order to be close to your friend.*

Zoey and Mike met each other last year when Mike moved in down the hall from her. He asked if he could steal her Wi-Fi password, and they've been friends ever since. Zoey can't believe how hot Mike is. Sometimes she blushes just looking at his picture, the one she has downloaded from his LinkedIn profile. Zoey knows that physically she's not Mike's type. He only dates athletic brunettes, and Zoey's neither of those things. But she hopes he'll make an exception to the rule, because he's always over and he tells her everything. In fact, he just broke up with his girlfriend and Zoey was the first person to hear about it. Mike works weekends, so Zoey watches his two dogs. They're so adorable, it doesn't really feel like work. She imagines that one day they'll be her dogs too. Zoey loves how comfortable Mike is around her. Last week, he asked her to do him a very personal favor. He handed her a razor and asked her to shave his back. His girlfriend used to do it for him, but since they broke up, he hasn't had anyone to help him get rid of the peach fuzz. Zoey felt so special that out of everyone he knew, he asked her to do it. Sometimes Mike bangs on her door after a night of drinking with his buddies and crawls into bed with her. Those are Zoey's favorite nights.

It may seem like Mike is using Zoey, but Zoey's using Mike too. Zoey gets to act out her fantasy of having an extremely hot boyfriend, while Mike gets someone to do his chores for him. This kind of friendship works for a little while, but eventually the chickens will come home to roost, sometimes in the form of a sporty brunette.

The Use is when your friend is using you for everything you're worth while you pretend you're in a real relationship, most of the time with someone you know is out of your league. Before you know it, you're paying their credit card bills, and even, in one case we know of, flying across the country to help them deliver their baby. Then one day, you will be slapped in the face with the fact that all this time and energy was a complete waste and this person would rather go out with a department store mannequin than you.

THE EMOTIONAL FRIENDSHIP
A friendship with deep emotional intimacy.

Kaylie and Eric are inseparable. Their friends call them Karic. Eric remembers everything about the day they met, April 11, 2007: the leopard leggings she was wearing, the freckles on her nose, the whole thing. Kaylie knows all his deepest darkest secrets—that he's afraid of earthquakes, that he wet the bed until he was eleven, and that any movie with Clint Eastwood makes him cry. And Eric knows everything about Kaylie's insecurities—that she gets really shy around guys she likes and she worries that her boobs are lop-sided. Many nights, they talk on the phone for two or three hours, until she falls asleep.

Sometimes Eric comes over and paints Kaylie's toenails. He would never tell his friends about this; they wouldn't let him live it down. But around her, he's not self-conscious. She makes him feel like he can tell her anything, be anything, and she'll accept him.

They did kiss once. It was the night she told him about her parents' divorce. She was crying so hard, and he kissed her face to take away the tears. Then he kissed her mouth. She pulled away and said she couldn't do that right now. They haven't talked about it since. He hopes she doesn't remember. But he does.

They talk about relationships all the time: why Eric has always gotten cheated on and why Kaylie finds it so hard to let her guard down around most guys. Eric can recite in chronological order all of Kaylie's previous boyfriends. But they never talk about the two of them dating. It's the ultimate taboo subject. He thinks about it all the time, sure. But they never talk about it.

Ugh, the cruelty of this friendship. Their souls are making love but their bodies are wearing chastity belts. It sucks. And it sucks for your prospective partners too. How can anyone compete with this person who knows you inside and out? This type of relationship is one of the hardest to change. When you're so in it, it's really hard to see that there's any damage being done. But there is. Because when you have such a strong emotional connection with someone else, you *should* be lovers. You treat each other as lovers would, but at the heart of it, you're just friends.

James and Tiana both started at an insurance company on the same day two years ago. There were five other newbies who started with them, but they all seemed kind of vanilla, so James and Tiana bonded from the very start. Now all their coworkers tease them about being office husband and wife. James rolls his eyes whenever they say this, but Tiana's heart beats faster, because she spends a lot of her downtime scribbling her first name with his last on her legal pad, even though she would never dream of taking a guy's last name. Maybe hyphenating, though. A typical day at work goes like this:

9 A.M.–10 A.M. James and Tiana instant message, filling each other in on what they did the night before. James describes the lame party he went to with his roommates; Tiana tells him how god-awful her friend's open-mic night was.

10:30 A.M. James stops by Tiana's desk and motions "Caffeine time!" She follows him into the office kitchen, where James gives her a jump drive full of his latest (illegally) downloaded music. He tells Tiana to pick her favorites and report back.

1 P.M. Tiana calls James (even though they're only ten cubicles apart) and asks what he's doing for lunch. He says he was planning on working through it. She convinces him to take a ten-minute break and get ramen with her. She's been craving it all week. James caves. Over lunch, they gossip about their coworkers and try to guess who in the office is hooking up.

3 P.M. James sends Tiana an Internet video of a cat wearing mittens and sliding all over the kitchen floor. Tiana responds with a video of a Maltipoo in a teacup.

4 P.M. Tiana's cubicle mate, Laura, asks her if James is single. Tiana responds in the affirmative. Laura asks if she'd mind if she went out with James. Tiana shrugs and says it's a free country, but she honestly doesn't think James likes dating people he works with. Tiana feels a major lump in her throat but tries to keep her cool.

6:30 P.M. James and Tiana take the elevator down to the parking garage. She tells him she liked all the hip-hop but none of the indie crap. He jokes that she has terrible taste in music. They stand outside of James's car for a few minutes as Tiana reenacts some really bad jokes from open-mic night. Then they go their separate ways. She never mentions the conversation she had with Laura.

And that's how it goes. During the workday, these two are inseparable. Only they never talk about anything serious or intimate. It's all fun jokey jokes and teasing each other. Tiana really wants to tell James how she feels, but she knows that could really mess up the good thing they've got going. They have to see each other for ten hours every day. If he turned her down, she could never look at him again. Tiana doesn't know what she'll do if Laura and James get together. She longs for the day when James gets a job at another company, because maybe then she could work up the courage to tell him how she feels. But for now, they're just office husband and office wife, till death do them part.

This kind of Friend Zone relationship has many added complications, because you have to see your friend all the time at work or school. What happens if things don't work out and you still have to face them? What if it's against office policy to date coworkers? What if you are working on a big project together and things get ugly? In our experience, when people work together or go to school together, they are especially afraid to put their feelings on the line, because there's nowhere to hide if things don't work out.

THE SOMETIMES WE HOOK UP
A friendship with occasional physical intimacy.

Jackson and Ali both work at a trendy fusion restaurant. They don't see each other at the restaurant that much because they have opposite shifts. But the entire staff hangs out at the bartender's house on Wednesday nights. It's become a time-honored tradition. Usually Ali spends the whole night flirting with the line cook, because he's one of those too-cool-for-school guys who wear ironic Members Only jackets. But every now and then, Ali gets pretty drunk and Jackson just happens to be at the right place at the right time. They've hooked up three times in the last year. Every time it happens, they don't mention it the next morning, aside from Ali mumbling, "Wow, I drank too much last night. Sorry, buddy." Jackson's afraid that if he brings it up, it won't happen again. He tries to keep his cool, but it's hard for him to look at Ali without seeing her pink lace bra in his head.

When Jackson finally does work up the courage to ask Ali out, she just gives a flustered smile and makes an excuse about being busy all weekend helping her friend move. In fact, if Jackson even mentions anything about dating or love, Ali changes the subject. They occasionally hang out one-on-one, going to a concert together or just getting some ice cream. When Jackson drives her home on those nights, he wonders if he should lean over and kiss Ali before she gets out of the car, but somehow it doesn't feel right.

This kind of relationship is a perfect example of what we like to call the Gray Area. It is confusing and indefinable. If a boyfriend-girlfriend relationship by definition involves physical intimacy, and a friend relationship is about an emotional connection without sex, then what happens when you're friends who are physically intimate but never talk about it or take it to the next level? That's the problem: you cling to the fact that there's physical intimacy to argue that you're not in the Friend Zone, when in actuality you are.

THE DATING BUT NOT DATING

A friendship where you see your friend one-on-one on a regular basis but you never move past the platonic point.

Matt and Sarah are dating. Well, kind of dating. They go out sometimes, but he never makes a move. They met in a weekend workshop for soapmaking, or something like that. Sarah can't really remember because at the time she was so depressed she was signing up for just about any self-enrichment workshop she could find. Now she just goes to the drugstore for her soap, and she and Matt are friends. Because they have no mutual friends (the other people in the class smelled like patchouli and sea algae), when they do go out, it usually looks and feels like a date. They are two people who go to the theater, eat Greek food, and talk about old Woody Allen movies. There is chemistry (at least Sarah thinks so), but neither of them has ever made a move, and there is no obvious flirting. They've never seen each other's apartments. They usually just meet out somewhere. They are dating but not dating. Anyone observing them when they're out would assume they are on a date. Why else would a guy see a community theater production of *Man of La Mancha*? Sarah wonders if Matt considers these practice dates for when he meets a real girl. The more nothing happens between them, the more she wonders why they're doing all this. Sarah likes Matt but doesn't know how he feels. She has no idea what's going on inside his head.

When you are in the Friend Zone, it's common to go on something that looks, feels, and sounds to other people like a date but in fact is not one. Therefore, you refer to this person as your friend, and so does your mom, who then starts to wonder about your sexuality. This fake date can only be kosher if both people are lonely and bored and have zero attraction to each other. However, if one person has real feelings for the other and hopes it will eventually turn into a real date, then it's Friend Zone territory. The fact that the other person has never made a move on you should make you wonder what you're doing in this nonsexual situation you've gotten yourself into.

THE ONLY LIKES YOU WHEN YOU'RE DATING SOMEONE ELSE
A friendship where you feel that the other person is only attracted to you when you're taken.

Katie and Sam are in the same circle of friends and have been close for some time now. They hang out a lot within the group, and sometimes at parties they can be found sitting on a couch fighting over who can text the fastest. Some of Sam's friends have told him to make a move. The problem is he has tried, in his own way, a couple of times, but Katie always brushes him off and makes a joke. Sam really likes Katie, but always figured she wasn't into him. Then he met Cara at his coed dodgeball tournament. She was pretty and nice and seemed to like him back. They started dating and things were going well.

At a party soon after Sam and Cara started seeing each other, Sam ran into Katie, who threw her arms around him and whispered that they needed to talk; she'd heard he was dating someone and wanted to know all about it. After hearing about Cara, Katie bad-mouthed her, even going so far as implying that Sam should break up with her because Cara wasn't right for him. Katie hinted that she was more his type. Sam thought that this was Katie's way of saying that she wanted to date him, so he broke things off with Cara the next day. He called Katie to tell her the news and suggest they go on a real date. She didn't pick up, so he left the message on her voice mail. Then something really weird happened: she never called him back. He finally received a text from her that said "Woot woot" but nothing more. At first he was confused and hurt. After all, he'd gotten out of a perfectly good relationship for Katie, and she wouldn't even pick up the phone when he called. But after talking to some of his friends, it hit him: maybe Katie was only interested in him when he was dating someone else.

This situation is insanely frustrating. A lot of times, your friend even tries to convince you to break up with your boyfriend/girlfriend only to blow you off as soon as you're single. One minute they give you hope, and the next you feel hopeless. Every time you're about to be happy, your friend blocks you.

Raffi and Kevin grew up in the same town in Florida. In high school, they dated during their senior year. This made sense, because he was in the band and she was on the flag team, which meant they spent a lot of time together after school. When they'd been dating for a year, Raffi "accidentally" hooked up with a visiting foreign exchange student from Australia. She felt awful about it and told Kevin, but he couldn't get over it, so they called it quits and went off to different colleges. Fast-forward fifteen years. Raffi has just moved back home from D.C., where she was working for a senator. And Kevin is coaching varsity baseball at their old high school. Raffi called Kevin the minute she got back into town, and they've been hanging out ever since. They go to the beach and play volleyball together. Sometimes it feels like things between them haven't changed since high school. None of the guys Raffi dated in D.C. were as funny as Kevin, who still calls her "Raffi Taffy," the nickname he gave her when they were dating.

Raffi's been on the verge of asking Kevin how he feels about her, but she always wimps out. They don't talk about their feelings much anymore. Kevin doesn't tell Raffi whether or not he's dating anyone. She teases him about all his other flings in an attempt to get something out of him, but he always just laughs and changes the subject. Raffi wants to tell him how sorry she is for what happened between them, that she's different now and that it would never happen again, but there never seems to be an opening, so instead, they just gossip about how fat and bald all the people they went to high school with have gotten.

This type of Friend Zone relationship is especially complicated, because it involves two people who at one point were actually dating. Should you be able to pick up right where you left off? Your friends probably tell you all the time that you should just go in for a kiss and see what happens. But it's not that simple. Since you broke up, you have each grown and changed in different ways. Just because you have made out with a person in the past doesn't guarantee you access to those lips for the rest of your life.

OKAY, YOU SEE YOURSELF IN ONE OF THESE STORIES. NOW WHAT?

Hopefully you found some similarities between your relationship with your friend and the people in these stories. If you didn't relate 100 percent, that's okay, but try to focus on the similarities, not the differences. Knowing what type of Friend Zone relationship you are in will help you know what to do to get out. The good news is, no matter what kind of relationship you're in, none of them are impossible to get out of. Now that you have identified the type of friendship you're in, you can finally begin to dig yourself out. And we are going to provide you with a big, fat, shiny shovel.

Dear Jet and Star,
My situation is really different from any-
one else's. I've known this girl my whole
life. We are family friends. We spend
every summer together and our moms
are practically sisters. She's always called
me her "brother from another mother,"
which used to be fine, but now it's really
starting to piss me off because I think I
like her. I used to think that Friend Zone
people had to meet when they are teen-
agers, and that you have to like the other
person from the beginning, but I guess
what I'm finding out now is that anyone
could get trapped. Even me!

CHAPTER 3

Assess Your Situation

Now that you've gotten a sense of what the Friend Zone looks like in action, it's time to face your own relationship head-on. We're going to take a good hard look at your "friendship" and see it for what it really is, in the cruel, cold light of day. We're going to ask you to take inventory like it's a department store after midnight. You'll look at what's there, what's missing, and what you're getting out of it. The point of this exercise is to leave the vagueness behind and step into the black-and-white truth of what's really going on.

If you were a soccer coach and your team was losing games left and right, you would sit down and try to figure out what happened. You would think to yourself, "How much did the team practice? What else was going on between the players? What stood in their way? What else could we have done to win?" We actually don't know if this metaphor is correct because we've never played sports in our lives, but we have watched *Bend It Like Beckham* a few times. On the next page, you are going to do your own Friendship Inventory and figure out what's really going on with you and your friend. Really do this. Make like the honors student that you are and fill this out!

Your Friendship Inventory

WHAT TYPE OF CONNECTION DO YOU HAVE?

Check below which kind of connection you have with your friend. You can check as many as apply, but remember: this is not your dream fantasy situation; we know you'd check 'em all. We're talking about what's *really there*. Ready? Go!

- **FUN** You have genuine fun together—you laugh and giggle, so much so that your stomach hurts after spending time together.

- **EMOTIONAL** You two are emotionally involved. You go to each other in times of need, and sometimes there's crying involved.

- **INTELLECTUAL** You are intellectually stimulated by each other, love to debate, and do things like go to museums, where you discuss the difference between Monet and Manet, etc.

- **PHYSICAL ATTRACTION** This one has to be mutual if you're going to check the box, because we know it's there on your side. Is there physical chemistry on both sides of the relationship, e.g., a lot of touching, hugging, cuddling, handholding, etc?

- **SPIRITUAL** You go to church together, or buddy up for yoga retreats, and afterward talk about the world and what's going to happen to you in the afterlife, etc.

WHAT ARE YOU GETTING OUT OF THIS FRIENDSHIP?

Check all that are true. Be honest.

- ☐ I get a pretend boyfriend/girlfriend.
- ☐ I get a warm and fuzzy feeling when we're together.
- ☐ I like being seen in public together.
- ☐ I like having a crush on them.
- ☐ I get an ego boost when we hang out.
- ☐ I like having someone to hang out with all the time.
- ☐ I like the fantasy that someday we will get together.
- ☐ They make me feel smart.
- ☐ They make me feel like a better person.
- ☐ They're fun to flirt with.
- ☐ I like the fact that other people talk about us and think we should be together.
- ☐ I like knowing that I know them better than anyone else.
- ☐ I like looking at them.
- ☐ I like hugging them and being affectionate.
- ☐ I like thinking that hanging out with them puts us in the same league.
- ☐ I like their group of friends.
- ☐ I like their family.
- ☐ I like having someone on my side.
- ☐ I like having sexual fantasies about them.
- ☐ I like to think about them before I go to sleep.
- ☐ I like feeling wanted/needed.

WHAT ARE YOU GIVING YOUR FRIEND?

- ■ I provide them with a fake boyfriend/girlfriend.
- ■ I drop everything to help out.
- ■ I provide emotional support.
- ■ I boost their ego.
- ■ I make them feel attractive.
- ■ I provide company when they are lonely.
- ■ I make them feel funny.
- ■ I drive them anywhere they want to go.
- ■ I pay for stuff.
- ■ I don't blow up at them when they cancel on me for other people.
- ■ I am their last-minute date.
- ■ I let them borrow my stuff.
- ■ I give them compliments.
- ■ I support their hopes and dreams.
- ■ I help them with their problems.
- ■ I make them feel smart.
- ■ I give them gifts.
- ■ I cheer them up if they feel sad.
- ■ I help out their friends.
- ■ I babysit their pets or their children. Even their plants.
- ■ I do things for them and expect nothing in return.

First look at the "What Type of Connection Do You Have?" section. You'll see that you rely on this person in some way (for fun, emotional support, or other reasons). In one way or another, you are connected to your friend on a meaningful level. There is a lot of good in your friendship; otherwise you wouldn't care so much about it. That's why there's potential for you to get out of the Friend Zone with this person: they share those connections too, and that puts both of you somewhere on the road to becoming real-life French kissers.

Now look at the "What Are You Getting Out of This Friendship?" section. Look at all those check marks! Being friends with this person has obviously added a lot to your life. On the surface, it looks like you're doing well here, but did you know that in a real relationship you could have all these things and a whole lot more? Sure, you get to long for someone, fantasize about them, and pine for them. Don't get us wrong: we know what a great feeling that is, at first. But you know what's infinitely better than that? When the other person feels exactly the same way you do.

Now let's look at the last section to see what you're giving your friend. As you can see, this is no two-way street. You are putting a whole lot into this relationship, and your friend is getting a pretty sweet deal. Go back and reread the list of boxes you just checked. Now think about it in reverse. Is your friend doing those same things for you? Most likely your answer is no. If you heard someone saying they were doing all those things with nothing in return, you would think they were pretty pathetic. But that pathetic person is you. You are the one giving it up for free and holding on to a fantasy of the two of you being together one day. It's almost like you are in a relationship with the fantasy and not with your friend. Only you can't hold hands with a fantasy at the movies, and you can't cuddle with a fantasy while drifting off to sleep. And you certainly can't make love to a fantasy. Why don't you just fantasize about your favorite movie star and save yourself a whole lot of heartache?

HOW DOES YOUR FRIEND FEEL ABOUT YOU?

Let's take a look at the other side of this coin. How does your friend really feel about you? Do they have fantasies about you too? Or has the thought of holding your hand never occurred to them, or worse yet, does it make their skin crawl? Take the "How Does Your Friend Feel About You" quiz at right to see where your friend stands. And don't cheat. There's really no point—it's only us.

So now you know how they feel about you right *now*, but one of the best things about feelings is they're not set in stone. They can change, and they do change all the time, and there's absolutely no reason why your friend can't change their mind about you. Now let's look at how your friend sees you, meaning what role you play for them in their life (See "How Does Your Friend See You?" on page 61).

When your friend looks at you, they see you in some way that is not boyfriend/girlfriend material, hence your place in the Friend Zone. Identifying *how* they see you in an honest way is crucial. If they see you as a sibling, or a parent, or a therapist, you've got an uphill climb. But again, it is possible to change that dynamic. If your friend sees you as a shadow, a human pillow, or a backup boyfriend/girlfriend, then they think you are too available and they most likely take your friendship for granted. The dynamic between the two of you needs to change, and we'll show you how very soon, don't worry. But first, before we do anything else, you need to ask yourself one very important question: Are you willing to risk it?

How Does Your Friend Feel About You?

HOW DOES YOUR FRIEND REACT WHEN YOU WALK INTO THE ROOM?

a. They light up like a Christmas tree.

b. They say "Hi" and give you a hug, but keep the focus on what they are doing.

c. They say "Hey" like you're their sibling, or they don't say anything at all.

WHEN YOU ASK THEM TO HANG OUT, THEY SAY...

a. "Yes," right away, no hesitation. They would forgo their grandma's eightieth to watch you brush your teeth.

b. That they are going to check their calendar and get back to you. Sometimes they say yes, sometimes they say no.

c. "Yes," then flake on you at the last minute because someone else asked them out.

WHEN YOU TOUCH THEM, THEY...

a. Touch you back or give you a big smile.

b. Let you touch them for a bit, then move away.

c. Cringe and walk away.

WHEN YOU CALL THEM, THEY...

a. Pick up on the first ring.

b. Pick up but then say they have to go, that they don't have time to talk.

c. Don't pick up but then text you later to see what you wanted.

WHEN YOU GET THEM ON THE PHONE, HOW DO THEY SOUND?

a. Excited and happy to hear from you.

b. Mellow; they are pretty tough to read sometimes.

c. Annoyed, or maybe just tired, like they just woke up from a nap.

THEY TALK ABOUT OTHER PEOPLE THEY LIKE...

a. Never.

b. Sometimes.

c. Constantly.

WHAT IS THE PERSONALITY OF THE PEOPLE YOUR FRIEND NORMALLY DATES?

a. Someone totally like you.

b. Someone who has some of your qualities.

c. Someone who is your exact opposite.

HOW OFTEN DO THEY MAKE PLANS WITH YOU?

a. All the time. Last night it was the movies, tomorrow it's a dodgeball tournament. They keep you really busy.

b. Every now and then. Whenever you start to think they don't want to hang out, they call you out of the blue.

c. Never. They're not very proactive, though.

Continued...

WHO IS YOUR FRIEND'S CELEBRITY CRUSH? (YOU CAN ASK THEM IF YOU DON'T KNOW.)

a. Someone people tell you looks like you.

b. Someone with the same coloring but different body type or vice versa.

c. Someone who's nothing like you in body, face, ethnicity, or personality.

DO THEIR FRIENDS PUSH YOU GUYS TO BE TOGETHER?

a. Yes, all the time; it's kind of annoying.

b. Some of them tease every now and then but are normally laughing.

c. No, never, why?

WHEN YOU GO UP TO THEM WHEN THEY'RE WITH THEIR FRIENDS, THEY ACT:

a. The same way they always do. They give you a hug and bring you into the group.

b. Depends. Sometimes they're really nice and sometimes they act like they don't know you.

c. They look down at the floor and pretend you don't exist.

RESULTS

Mostly As: They're Dying for You to Make a Move
Your friend has been waiting for you to do something since the 1960s. They're open and ready for something to happen between you two. Now you just have to go for it, which is easier said than done, we know. In the coming chapters we'll help you turn this little spark of attraction into a full-blown wildfire. You are really close to getting out of the Friend Zone and into their pants (or skorts, or whatever they wear).

Mostly Bs: You Need to Get Their Attention
Your friend may be interested in you, but you are too easy for them. They like a bit of a challenge. Your friend is running hot and cold with you because they're not sure how they feel about you. Some days they only see you as a friend; some days they think they want something more. Our job is to help you convince them that they do want to date you. We are going to stop this whole hot-and-cold thing and switch it to hot all the time. We're going to help you play the game a little better, so that they will see you as an attractive person and not just their buddy.

Mostly Cs: You Have a Challenge
Your friend doesn't know you're alive, or they're not currently attracted to you—or maybe it just hasn't occurred to them yet. This is the hardest row to hoe. So yes, it's going to take some work, but we have faith in you. The biggest challenge will be to get them to see you in a completely different light. Lucky for you, that is what the rest of this book is about. Stick with us and we'll show you how to present yourself in a completely different way.

How Does Your Friend See You?

- ■ **PARENT** When your friend is drunk, they call you to ask for a ride home. If they need a little extra money to pay their rent, they come to you. You may have even done their laundry or grocery shopping a few times.

- ■ **SIBLING** You are super-extremely familiar with each other. You know too much about each other. There is no real flirting going on.

- ■ **BACKUP BOYFRIEND/GIRLFRIEND** You do everything a normal boyfriend or girlfriend would do. You pick them up from the airport, give them presents, and put their happiness above your own.

- ■ **HUMAN PILLOW** Your friend is very affectionate toward you. You sometimes spend the night at their house and hold each other. People think you're together because you're all over each other.

- ■ **SHADOW** You're always around them. You see your friend almost every day of the week. You go on mundane errands with them. You have a key to their place or know where the spare is.

- ■ **THERAPIST** You are their shoulder to cry on. Your friend calls you at 3 A.M. to vent about whatever drama they've been going through all night, and you pick up the phone. You count and recount your friend's life events, without so much as a "How was your day?" from them.

ARE YOU WILLING TO RISK IT?

Julie loved Graham. She loved him so much that when she blew out the candles on her cake, she couldn't think of anything except "I wish Graham loved me." Julie constantly thought of him and wanted things to go to the next level, but she never wanted to make any actual changes to achieve her goal. She pretty much liked things the way they were. She loved hanging out with him and listening to old Cure songs together. She liked daydreaming about him flipping his shaggy hair. Graham dated on and off, usually preppy girls who had no idea what they were talking about when it came to the things Julie and Graham enjoyed, like Morrissey and dive bars.

Then one day, Julie noticed that Graham was talking a lot about Allison, a new girl in his apartment building. He told her that Allison had really good taste in music and sang in an awesome band, and that they'd spent the previous night laughing and talking about touring together that summer, which really annoyed Julie. Graham was supposed to be saving himself for her! Then it hit her: she was in the Friend Zone, and unless she really risked something, she would stay there. Julie realized she didn't want him to be with Allison—she wanted him to be with her. Allison wasn't Graham's soul mate; Julie was. At the end of the day, it would be far worse to watch Graham and Allison send out their wedding invitations than to risk their friendship and tell Graham how she felt. She had always believed that their friendship was the most important thing in the world, but now she realized the chance to be his girlfriend was even more important, and she was about to lose her shot.

We know exactly what you're thinking: "Oh no! The friendship, what will happen to the friendship?" Well, we think that's a boatload of donkey crap. What you're really thinking deep down is: "I'm afraid my friend will reject me and then I'll never want to show my face to them again." True, if you put yourself out there and get shot down, you may be too embarrassed to ever talk to your friend again. But we think the whole save-the-friendship thing is just an excuse, so you don't have to feel bad for not doing what you really want to do. What you're actually afraid of is rejection and loss. We all are, but anything worth having is going to cost you.

First, let's step back for a minute and think about what you are really risking: fantasy. The one where you two are together forever and are the best couple who ever lived, where you don't fight and are having constant sexual intercourse for the rest of your lives. This is also, coincidentally, all part of the same fantasy where you don't have to lift a finger and your friend suddenly comes to their senses all on their own. Out of the blue, your friend is struck by how irresistibly attractive you are. They fall at your feet begging you to go apartment hunting together. It's hard to let go of this fantasy, because it's your security blanket. The problem is, your fantasy is not reality. It's the thing you go to in the middle of the night; it's your religion. The church of One-Day-Soon-We'll-Get-Together-and-Then-My-Life-Will-Be-Perfect. Hallelujah, Amen! But riddle us this: what will keep you warmer at night—your dreams of being with your friend, or the heat from a real live body sleeping next to you?

Every Friend Zone relationship has a shelf life. You can't live in this fuzzy gray area forever, and you won't. Eventually someone jumps ship, and it probably won't be you. So if it's going to end sometime, it might as well be on your terms and when you can give it a real shot. What we're saying is: you don't live forever, so make a move while you still have blood coursing through your veins.

Maybe you've already decided. Maybe you haven't gotten there yet. Once you put your feelings on the line, there's no going back. Whatever you two had going on before is going to be different once you say that you like them as more than a friend. You can't unscramble an egg. So are you ready to take the plunge and go through the steps ahead and jump in the pool already? It's so hot outside, isn't it? Or would you rather not, because your "friend-ship" is too important? Is your weekly torturefest—that is, pizza and bowling night—really worth preserving?

Ask yourself this: Do you want to live in faith or fear? You can't live in both. Being willing to lose what you have right now may lead to your biggest gain. Who wants to see a movie where someone is in love with their friend but never says anything, never changes anything about themselves or takes a risk? No one. We all want to see that person laying it on the line. But if that's not you and you really do need a racquetball partner more than a sexual one, then stop right now. You're right—you're not ready to risk it.

If you haven't noticed, we are always going to err on the side of the risk. There is nothing more fun in life than doing what you really want to do, deep in your heart, without fear, knowing that either way, you will be a better version of yourself in the end: the one who says what they feel and then gets the person of their dreams, or at least can move on and meet the actual person of their dreams. Remember, the one who you're really meant to be with is *dying* to be with you; the other is just an impostor.

✦✦✦✦✦✦✦✦

Hey WG:

I've been in the dreaded Friend Zone for a long time now. A really, really long time. I've thought about laying down an ultimatum with my friend and telling him how I really feel, but I'm so scared that if I do that, it will ruin everything. I used to think I'd rather at least have him in my life as a friend rather than nothing at all. But now, I feel like I have to do something! My life is passing me by while I wait for him to come around. We're hanging out this weekend and I'm going to tell him how I feel. Wish me luck!

✦✦✦✦✦✦✦✦

CHAPTER 4
The Confession

Does your friend know how you feel about them? "Well, they should. Isn't the fact that I knit them a coffee cozy for Christmas a dead giveaway?" You would think so, but we're not talking about actions, or hints, or secret messages. It's easy for your friend to write off the "signs" that you've given them. Maybe they should know you like them because you've sat through every single one of their water polo practices, and they know how much you hate the smell of chlorine. But in your friend's head, you're just a really great friend. If you've never told your friend explicitly how you feel about them—that you like them, as *more* than a friend—then *please*, for God's sake, assume that they don't know.

So, have you already told your friend how you feel? Before you say yes, answer these questions: Did you clearly tell your friend "I like you as more than a friend and I want to date you"? Did you get a real answer? Were both of you sober at the time? If you can honestly answer yes to all of these questions, then good for you—you can skip right ahead to the next chapter. But most of you reading this haven't confessed, or you didn't do it the right way. That's what this chapter is for: to show you exactly what to say and how to say it so that your friend knows beyond the shadow of a doubt how you feel about them. It's time to start your journey out of the Friend Zone, and the first step is the Confession.

There are many different ways to confess, and we're going to tell you exactly how to do it, but first, it might be helpful to look at some examples of confessions that didn't work and see what went wrong.

THE HALFWAY CONFESSION

Alex and Tricia had been friends for two years. Her cousin had introduced them, and they hit it off right away. Alex had a major crush on Tricia, but he never thought she would go for him. He saw her as way out of his league. Plus, she normally dated athletic guys, and he was the furthest thing from a jock. Still, Tricia's cousin kept pushing him to tell her how he felt about her. Alex didn't want to, because he hates serious discussions, and he gets really nervous and sweaty every time he has to talk about something important. Tricia's cousin said he should tell her over instant message, because they spent a ton of time on it anyway, so it made sense. One day, while Alex and Tricia were IMing, he worked up the courage and typed, "Hey, I know this is stupid, but have you ever thought about dating me?" Her response took forever. He refused to blink as he stared at the screen, waiting for her to write back. When she finally did, she replied with "LOL. What kind of question is that?" He backed down right away with "LOL. Never mind." He never tried again, and to this day, they're still good friends, but Alex has no idea how Tricia actually feels about him.

Alex made a couple of serious mistakes in his confession. First, he told Tricia over the computer and not face-to-face. A successful confession has to be done in person. That's the only way to make sure your friend is listening and taking you seriously. You have to be able to read body language and see facial expressions when you confess. Plus, by telling her how he felt over the computer, it diminished the strength of his feelings for her. Shouldn't something as important as your love for someone be expressed in person and not over a computer screen? Also, Alex never got a real answer from Tricia because he didn't push for one. He dropped the subject right away and backed off, and never even got to find out how she felt about him. All of Alex's stressing over his confession was for nothing, because he didn't do it right to begin with.

THE OVER-THE-TOP CONFESSION

Zola has liked Riley since the day she met him. It was the second week of college, and she saw him in line at the student union. He was buying a school sweatshirt to send to his brother, and he asked Zola for her opinion. Ever since then, Zola's been head over heels. All of her roommates have been getting on her to do something about it, warning her that if she doesn't take some action soon, she'll be in the Friend Zone forever. They say that Riley likes her too, but he's so laid back and clueless, if anyone's going to make a move, it has to be her. At first, Zola ignored her roommates. She's kind of old-fashioned and has always thought that the guy should be the one to make the first move. But last week, when Riley stopped by on his way to go surfing and she saw him looking tan and muscular in his swim trunks, she decided she didn't want to wait around anymore. She needed to do something to tell him how she felt about him. And it needed to be *big*.

Zola and Riley were in astronomy together. Normally during class, they barely paid attention. The class was held in a huge lecture hall, so they could play hangman or draw fake tattoos on each other without getting caught. But today Zola needed Riley's full attention to be on her during her presentation. Zola stood in front of the room, trying to slow her beating heart. She was supposed to be presenting on recent discoveries in space, but she had decided to slip in a surprise slide just for Riley. After talking about the new stars and celestial objects that had been mapped out, Zola said that the most important discovery was a new planet. She pressed a button and a slide came up onscreen that said "Planet Riley." From across the massive lecture hall, she saw Riley's mouth gape open. Zola's voice quivered as she explained that Planet Riley's gravitational pull was so strong that nothing could escape it. Then she took a breath, looked Riley square in the eye and said, "And that's why, Riley, I can't help but spend every day orbiting you." The room went silent. Riley's face turned bright red, and he looked like he wanted to bury himself in his hoodie. All the students in the lecture hall turned around to look at him. Zola could hear people giggling around her. She couldn't breathe. Riley sprang from his chair and sprinted out of the room. Zola barely had time to blink. She stood there, listening to the laughter mixed with the gasps from the other students. She would have given anything to have a hole in the earth open up and swallow her completely.

The problem with this confession was that it was too much of a shock. Riley had no clue how Zola felt about him, and then to be hit with it all at once in such a big way was too much for him to process. It also happened in front of a crowd, so the stakes were too high. A confession shouldn't be the same as throwing a surprise birthday party for someone. The goal is not to catch the person off-guard and knock their socks off. The goal is to gently let them know how you feel and find out how they feel about you. The fewer fireworks, violins, and general hoopla, the better. It needs to be about you and your friend, not about the crazy, huge, grand gesture that you pulled off. Those things are great for romantic comedies but tend not to work as well in real life.

Confession Don'ts

- DON'T CONFESS WHILE INTOXICATED.
- DON'T CONFESS OVER THE COMPUTER.
- DON'T CONFESS OVER THE PHONE.
- DON'T CONFESS IN FRONT OF A CROWD.
- DON'T LEAVE UNTIL YOU GET AN ANSWER.

HOW TO CONFESS THE RIGHT WAY

There are many ways to begin the Confession. Basically, all that needs to come out of the conversation is for you to tell your friend how you feel about them and to get a response letting you know how they feel about you. Pretty simple stuff. But getting into it is the hardest part. You don't want to come out of the blue with, "Yeah, that sucks that you dropped your cell phone in the toilet. . . . Anyway, I really like you." So read the following to see what kind of confession best suits your relationship.

THE FUN AND FRIENDLY CONFESSION

Brianne and Seth worked at a really hip commercial production company, the kind with pool tables and beanbag chairs. Brianne was a production coordinator, and Seth was a set builder who went from company to company but had worked with Brianne for the last four jobs. He and Brianne had a very similar sense of humor and would joke and laugh all day long. Brianne always had a thing for Seth. He was so funny and down-to-earth and knew how to build things. Most of the guys she'd met in the business were ego-driven control freaks afraid to get their hands dirty. Unfortunately, Brianne was in the Friend Zone. Seth often referred to her as his little sis. If people in the office said they should date, he always laughed it off. They'd never gotten very deep, so Brianne didn't want to scare him with an emotional confession. They had a fun, friendly relationship, and so she knew her confession would have to fit in with that. She couldn't sit him down to explain that she'd liked him for years and thought about registering for their wedding every night before she went to sleep. At the same time, she didn't want to just mention it and have him laugh it off and still never know if he liked her or not. She needed to keep it light but still find out how he felt.

She decided to bring it up when they did their morning "who could get the most crap in their cereal" competition in the office kitchen. Seth was pouring a bag of gummy bears into his bowl when Brianne grabbed the rest and threw them in hers. "Hey!" he said, reaching for the bag. Brianne smiled at him. They were always teasing each other. Brianne decided it was now or never. "You know, in the past, when I liked a guy, I would kick him or rip up his drawings. Now I do that with you! I haven't changed a bit. I have no game when it comes to a crush."

❖ ❖ ❖ ❖ ❖ ❖

Brianne judged her audience very well. When you have a fun relationship that isn't too deep, you don't want your confession to be any heavier than your normal conversations with your friend. You like them. That's a fact, just like your ability to kick their ass at dodgeball any day of the week. Those two things should have just as much value. With fun relationships, your main objective is to put your feelings out there in the same way you always talk to them, but in a more direct manner. Don't be afraid of being bold, either. If your tone is fun and playful, then you can get away with serious statements. Saying, "Uhhh, I love you so much" in a playful manner will go further than sitting this person down, getting very serious and saying, "Uhhh, I love you so much" as you stare into their eyes, sweating bullets. If your relationship is less competitive and more positive, you might say, "You are the coolest person ever, when are we gonna get married? Seriously?" And then you might say, "I'm serious, why don't we date?" Sometimes, the more direct, the better. Just remember to say how you feel and ask them how they feel about you. Your own relationship up to this point will dictate your tone and how out there you want to be with your confession.

THE CASUAL RELATIONSHIP CONFESSION

Joanna and Philip knew each other through church, where they were both leaders of the youth group. They supervised the junior congregation's volunteer outings, like collecting food for low-income families or serving breakfast at homeless shelters. Philip looked forward to going to church on Sunday mornings because it meant he'd get to see Joanna. He thought she was the prettiest woman he'd ever laid eyes on. When she smiled at him, he felt like his whole face got red. He'd wanted to tell her how he felt for a while. He knew he was in the Friend Zone, but he thought if she knew how he felt, things would be different. He'd lie awake at night, having whole conversations with her in his head, fantasizing about asking her out and telling her how special she was. The problem was that whenever they were together, they were focusing on the task at hand. They were helping the youth group plan the annual church picnic, or chaperoning the trip to the amusement park. They didn't see each other outside of church, so they never really got to talk about the nature of their relationship. That would be weird in front of the kids.

Joanna and Philip knew each other on a casual level. He knew that she loved to go hiking and that she dreamed of going on a mission trip to Africa one day, but he didn't know a lot about her past relationships or what she looked for in a boyfriend. And he'd never really told her what his type was or that he was tired of dating around and ready to settle down. But Philip knew he had to take some action. He couldn't sit through one more of Reverend Baxter's sermons trying not to breathe in Joanna's perfume. So, after the youth group meeting on Friday, Philip walked Joanna to her car. Their hands were full of the donated items that they were dropping off at the women's shelter. They talked about their plans for the weekend, as they normally did after the youth group meeting. When Joanna asked what he was up to, Philip answered, "Well, I'm not really sure. I spend all week looking forward to seeing you on Fridays, so I don't really plan beyond that. I know we don't talk every day, but when I'm with you, I am so happy."

Philip knew he had to bite the bullet and acknowledge that his confession was going to seem out of the blue. Since in a casual relationship you don't talk about love, you can't get too mushy with your friend. That will scare them away. You have to keep the confession casual, as in, "I like what I know about you so far and I want to know more." You don't know everything there is to know about this person, so you can only speak to what you do know—that you enjoy the time you have together, and that you like how you feel when you're with them. And then you have to find out if your friend shares your feelings or not. In a casual relationship, you may not be very deep in the Friend Zone, but you're headed there, so you have to confess your feelings before too much time goes by. It's never going to seem natural to go into the Confession in a relationship like this, so it's best to just acknowledge that it's a little awkward or hard for you to do, and then just go for it.

THE SERIOUS/EMOTIONAL CONFESSION

Brad and Sue met in AA. They spent their nights in the meetings talking about what drove them to the program and how to live life to the fullest now that they were sober. After the meeting, they would usually go out with other AA friends for a meal at the diner next door. They would talk the night away, sometimes laughing, sometimes crying. They all knew each other inside and out. Some nights they would talk at a coffee shop until two in the morning, just spilling their guts. Sue would tell Brad about the guys she was dating, and Brad would tell her what he thought was happening from a guy's perspective. They totally trusted each other and were always 100 percent honest . . . except for one little thing. Brad was completely in love with Sue. At first he didn't think much of her, other than that she was another cool person he'd met in AA. Then it grew the more they talked and the more he got to know her. Everyone knew he was in the Friend Zone.

Sue dated a lot of AA guys but always said Brad was her best guy friend, and she wouldn't trade that for the world. Brad was beginning to feel guilty not telling her the truth about how he felt. He loved her and couldn't stomach hearing one more thing about a guy who couldn't even string two words together. He felt Sue was having fun with these immature guys and then using Brad as her pretend boyfriend. They had such a deep connection that he knew he had to be honest and sincere when he told her his true feelings. He also had to apologize for not telling her sooner and explain it was something that had been growing. He knew that whatever came from it, it was better than sitting on the sidelines and watching her kiss another guy.

On Friday night, after the AA meeting, everyone usually went to their friend Rick's house to soak in his hot tub and watch movies on his huge flat-screen. Everyone looked forward to it, especially Brad and Sue. They always found a corner to themselves and sipped tea and analyzed everyone in the room, but tonight Brad was going to focus on Sue and Sue alone. He started by saying, "I want you to know I have romantic feelings for you. I think you are a wonderful person, and you're really beautiful. I'm sorry for not saying something sooner, but I didn't know if my feelings would pass. Now I know they probably won't, so I need to be honest. I can't be your friend, because I want to be your boyfriend." Sue looked puzzled. "You do?" Then he said, "Yes, I do. And I need to know if you have feelings for me."

Brad knew that he couldn't just mention to Sue that he liked her out of nowhere and not explain more than that. They'd spent hours discussing the parent/child dynamics they grew up with, the problems with their past relationships, the difference between love and lust, and other such topics. To not go in a little deeper with the Confession would be jarring. With the Emotional Friendship, the other person needs to feel safe. They've told you everything, so you don't want them to feel you're keeping anything back. At the same time, you don't want to overwhelm them with too much information, such as, how long specifically you've felt like this, or every undying dream you've had for your life with them. Above all, you don't want to use the word *love*, even if that's how you feel. Keep to the present moment as much as you can, while acknowledging the feelings that have grown. Be honest and direct but sensitive to the fact that they might be a little taken aback, or even angered by your confession. With the emotional relationship, give them time to process your confession, but at the same time, don't let them off the hook for an answer.

THE BRAINY CONFESSION

Beth and Chip were both assistant professors at the University of Indiana. She taught in the psychology department, and he did genetics research, but when they weren't holed up in their offices, they could be found walking through campus together. They ate lunch side by side almost every day, unless one of them had a department meeting. When Chip hit a roadblock with his research on the genetic makeup of yeast, Beth was the first person he called to give him a pep talk. And when she found out her article on the link between stress relief and probiotics was going to be published, Chip was the first person to take her out to celebrate. Several times, a colleague of Beth's would see them together on campus and later come up to ask her if Chip was her boyfriend.

Beth always blushed and said, "No, he's just a friend," but she secretly got a little thrill from knowing that they seemed like a couple. Beth could think of nothing that she would like more than to be Chip's girlfriend. She could see it all so clearly: the two of them on the couch on Sunday morning, reading the paper. He would have the Science & Technology section and she would get Health & Medicine.

Beth often laughed at herself, because she should be better at this. Psychology was her expertise. Why couldn't she just get inside Chip's brain and figure out how he felt about her? But Chip didn't make it easy. Their conversations were so intellectual. They could spend hours debating human development, but they almost never talked about feelings. Sure, Chip was able to break down the common traits in all of Beth's past boyfriends. He told her she had a proclivity for "codependent alpha males." But he never let on if his brain released a little extra dopamine when she was around. If only she could get him in the lab and attach him to a heart monitor.

One night, Chip came over to Beth's apartment. After one of their intellectually stimulating discussions about why autism is more prevalent among males, Beth took a long sip of her wine and said, "I have a question for you." "Shoot," Chip answered. "Can men and women have truly platonic friendships?" Beth asked.

Beth handled this situation perfectly. By bringing up the subject on an intellectual level, she opened the door for them to talk about their own relationship. Beth made love an intellectual issue as well. If you have a friendship like this, where you spend the majority of your time debating weighty issues, then you should treat your confession as just another stimulating topic. But make sure you do eventually steer the conversation toward your actual feelings. If you don't, you could have a whole argument about the nature of friendship and never make it personal. You need to use the question as an entry point to reveal your true feelings for your friend and find out how they feel about you. Make sure you tell them how you feel about them, as scary as that can be, and get them to reveal what they've been feeling as well. Just because you two normally have a meeting of the minds doesn't mean that your hearts can't powwow as well.

BUT, BUT, BUT... WHAT IF MY FRIEND IS IN A RELATIONSHIP WITH SOMEONE ELSE?

You are still in the Friend Zone, even if your friend is currently in a relationship. Your friend still looks to you to fill the void that their significant other is not filling. In this scenario, you have to ask yourself an additional question: Is it safe to hit on this person, or will you get punched in the face? Love makes people do crazy things, so remember to tread lightly. And don't bad-mouth your friend's significant other in the process. Obviously, there is something about them that your friend likes, so don't insult them or compare the two of you, because you may not win. Instead, leave the current boyfriend or girlfriend out of the conversation.

During the Confession, tell your friend, "Look, I know you're in a relationship right now and I respect that, but I think we have really good chemistry. If you guys ever break up, I would love to go out with you. But until then, I can't sit around and watch you date someone else." Then you start the Separation, which we'll talk about in the next chapter and which will last as long as their relationship does. You have to go full-speed into meeting and dating other people at this point, so you're not just waiting around for them to break up with their boyfriend or girlfriend. When they do break up, if you're not already in a more fulfilling relationship, proceed to Chapter 8: The Kill, and take it from there.

BUT WHAT IF I'M INTO A BEST FRIEND'S EX?

Before the Confession, you should stop and think about how important this person is to you. Is this just a crush that will be over by New Year's? Or do you think you'll be swapping wedding bands in a few short years? If and only if you think this is for real, then you need to go talk to your best friend. You have to be honest with them and tell them about your feelings for their ex, and then ask permission to date their sloppy seconds. If they are completely over their ex, they'll probably give their blessing and you can be on your merry way, but just know that down the road, your best friend may have a change of heart, so you must prepare yourself for that, to some extent.

When friends share lovers, there's always a lot more drama. Your best friend might say they're cool with it, and then eight months later, as you and their ex are slow dancing together to "Lady in Red," your best friend could be crying alone in a bathroom. If your feelings for this person are lukewarm and you're not sure you see forever in their eyes, then don't do it. It's not worth messing up a lifelong friendship for a person you're only kind of into. Proceed with caution.

YOUR FRIEND'S RESPONSE

There are two possible responses to "I like you. Do you like me?": "Yes" and everything else. If you get a resounding, enthusiastic, jumping-up-and-down "HELL YES!" then congratulations, you're one of the privileged few. You can skip ahead to chapter 9, you lucky bastard. If you get any other response: a "Maybe," an "Umm...I don't know," a weird look, a "Maybe but I have to think about it," then keep chugging along on the How-to-Get-out-of-the-Friend-Zone Express. Know that this is completely expected and you are on the right track.

MOVING FORWARD

The Confession puts you on your way to getting out of the Friend Zone. As scary and uncomfortable as it is, you have to do it if you ever want to change your current situation. Even if you got a "No, I don't feel the same way," it's okay, because a "no" today is not necessarily a "no" tomorrow. These things take time. You have to plant the seed first, and then give it time and space to grow until it becomes a full-grown flower of lust for your hotness. It takes a while to come around to change. People will always be resistant at first, so don't be shocked if your friend is thrown off by the Confession. After all, you are admitting something that could potentially lead to a lot of change for both of you.

Now that you've gotten the Confession over with, you can truly begin your journey. The Confession is the beginning of the process, but it's not something that you should expect any real results from, because you haven't done any of the hard work yet. Yes, it gets harder, but it also gets easier at the same time. You've put your heart on the line. It's done; you don't have to obsess about it anymore. You've gotten your answer, and now you can finally move forward. All the stewing and waiting and fantasizing are over. Now is the time to get off the couch and out of the Friend Zone forever.

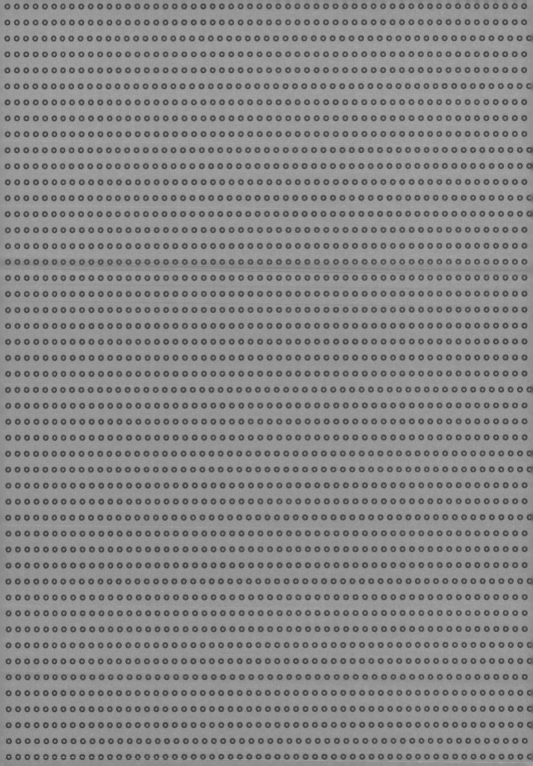

Part Two

. . . .

GETTING OUT

CHAPTER 5

The Separation

The Separation is a set period of time where you intentionally remove yourself from contact with your friend. In other words, you "back the truck up." It's almost like you are going on vacation to a place where there is no cell phone reception or Wi-Fi. You are taking yourself out of the "friendship" for a while so that you can work on yourself. During this period you will have little to no contact with your friend.

WHY SEPARATE?

We know what you're thinking. You hate this part. You want to scream and cry and kick your legs and say, "No! I can't!" Well, crack addicts hate to stop doing crack, too. You're thinking, "If I'm not always in their face, they'll forget about me," when in fact the exact opposite is true. The more you're out of the picture, the more your friend will be thinking of you. It's like that beautiful piece of art at your parents' house. You don't see it because you've been staring at it your whole life. It takes someone else coming in and pulling it off the wall for you to even notice it existed, let alone how fabulous it is. That's what the Separation is for: to force your friend to realize what life is like without you and stop taking you for granted.

"Why the Separation? Isn't that a little dramatic? Can't I just sit on my doorstep and wait for my friend to come around and see me for the sexual, attractive, perfect partner that I am?" Here's the deal. No one comes around on their own. You've been doing the same thing all along (that is, *nothing*), and that hasn't been working very well for you. So why not try it our way (that is, the *right* way)? In case you need some more convincing, here are a few other reasons why you need to go through the Separation.

You're always in your friend's face, so how can they miss you? They can't. They see you all the time, so they don't have to think to themselves: "I wonder what so-and-so is up to" or "I wish so-and-so were here" (in this example, you are so-and-so). Your friend needs time away from you so they can really reflect on your worth. Your friend needs to realize they love spending time with you, and the only way they can do that is by missing you.

Your friend takes you for granted. When you were a kid, did you sit around and thank your lucky stars that your mom always bought your favorite cereal? No, because you took her for granted. That's how your friend sees you, as someone they will always have around, no matter how they behave. Your friend sees you as an unconditional family member and hasn't ever really considered the fact that you may not want to do their laundry. They don't care about you because they don't think about you. Your friend knows they can mistreat you and you will come right back to them, because that's how it has always worked in the past. Look at a couple you really admire—they value and respect each other. Your friend doesn't value and respect you, and they're not going to until you make them.

Your friend needs to picture their life without you. Do you ever have those fantasies where your friend is crying at your funeral? Or maybe they see you in a hospital bed and finally realize they love you? Your instincts are right—your friend does need to see their life without you, but you don't need to die to get there. They just need to think they've lost you, so they'll reassess why they like having you around, and why they need you in their life. Sometimes you don't know what you've got until it's gone.

Your friend needs to admire you. They need to look at you and be in awe of you, and they can't do that if you are an appendage. Every good relationship is built on mutual admiration, and right now the admiration in your relationship is one-sided. Your friend can't really see you when you're always there. They need to see you in your glory, and you can't show them that from inside their lower intestine. They need to look at you from afar and think you are amazing and wonderful . . . because you are.

Your friend wants a chase! Everyone likes a pursuit, and your friend won't get one if you're always an inch away. Your friend wants to feel a sense of accomplishment about winning you over, not like you just fell out of the sky and into their lap. They want a chase, so give it to them.

WHY YOU'RE SCARED

"But If I'm not in the picture, my friend will forget who I am!" You're afraid that all this work you've put in to being a good friend will be in vain if you walk away right now. You worry that if you're not clinging to them every single minute, reminding them how amazing you are, that they'll turn around and get with someone else, someone who's not as good and worthy and kind as you are. You'd rather have shreds of dignity than all of it. You'll accept scraps! We get it, it's scary. Change is hard. It's painful, even. But the Separation is necessary. Sometimes that bad/evil part of yourself, the destructive messed-up part, wants you to stay where it's safe and never get what you really want. But the best part of yourself is the one that says, "Please, please do this. You only live once, and I'm sick of this situation!" Now is the moment you have to choose to live in fear or to be brave. Choose brave.

HOW TO DO IT

Now we are going to walk you through the Separation, step by step.

STOP INITIATING CONTACT

Think about the last week. How many times have you been the first one to call, or text, or approach your friend? You probably do it without even thinking. Remember that movie you went to see last weekend, the one where you two sat side by side in the dark and the whole time all you could think about was doing that terrible move where you yawn and put your arm on their shoulder? Well, whose idea was that movie? It was yours, wasn't it? And you did the inviting, and you got the tickets a day in advance and smuggled in Sour Patch Kids in your back pocket because that's your friend's favorite candy, even though it rips up the roof of your mouth. It's all you, it's always all you, and your friend doesn't have to lift a finger. Well, not anymore. From now on, you will not be the first one to engage. This means you will adopt a set of rules and stick to them.

You will want to continue doing these things. That's why the Separation is so hard. You'll think about doing these things all the time.

The Rules

- I WILL NOT TEXT MY FRIEND FIRST.
- I WILL NOT MESSAGE MY FRIEND OR USE ANY FORM OF SOCIAL MEDIA TO CONTACT THEM.
- I WILL NOT INSTANT MESSAGE MY FRIEND.
- I WILL NOT CALL MY FRIEND.
- I WILL NOT WAIT FOR MY FRIEND AFTER SCHOOL OR AT WORK.
- I WILL NOT INVITE MY FRIEND OUT TO EVENTS.
- I WILL NOT STOP BY MY FRIEND'S PLACE TO SAY HI ON MY WAY HOME.
- I WILL NOT WALK UP TO MY FRIEND AND SAY HELLO.

But then you'll find other things to do. You have been addicted to your friend's company. You cling to your nightly 11 P.M. text fest because it's comfortable and makes you feel close to them. Just because it feels good doesn't mean it's good for you. Alcoholics feel pretty good with a bottle of booze in their hand, too.

You must stop all communication. Completely. If you do it only halfway, say, texting them once an hour instead of your usual five times, then nothing is going to change. There is no gray area here. It's cold turkey, baby. So make the decision right now that you are in this to win this. You are running the whole marathon at full speed. You are getting to the finish line. That's the only way to make your friend notice that anything's changed between the two of you. And believe us, you do want your friend to notice.

WHAT TO DO IF...

Your friend calls you a lot: You can pick up every once in a while, but only between the hours of noon and 6 P.M. You say, "Hey, I'm running out the door, what's up? Are you okay?" and then after two minutes, you say you have to go and hang up, even if your friend tries to get you to stay on the phone. But 80 percent of the time, let it go to voice mail. Don't push "ignore," because your friend will know when you've ended the call.

Your friend doesn't stop texting you: Only text back during your new normal business hours of noon and 6 P.M. No late-night texts. *None!* When your friend does text you, wait at least an hour to text back, depending on when they first texted. Reply with short answers but keep it semi-friendly, for example: "Oh, sounds cool. Sorry I can't, next time!" Don't open texts after business hours, because some phones can see when texts have been read.

Your friend keeps inviting you out: If your friend invites you out, you can't go. *Period.* You're washing your hair. You cannot see your friend during this time. Remember, you're on your "friendcation," and this includes not going to a place you know they'll be. That's cheating. If you don't fully commit to the process, you aren't giving it a real chance.

Your friend messages and e-mails you: Everyone wants to get into a fight over e-mail. Wait at least twenty-four hours, reply with a few words, like, "Hey, everything's fine here, glad to hear you're okay! Let's talk soon." If the e-mail is dramatic, you must ignore it or respond with a simple "Hey, sorry you're going through all that, but I'm just really overwhelmed with other things. This is not about you. I hope you're okay!"

Your friend keeps coming up to talk to you: Keep it very brief. You have somewhere to be or something to do. You can't engage with your friend. If they try to get into it, just tell them you've got to run, then smile and say, "I'll see you later." Never apologize for being unavailable, and don't get into why you don't want to have a discussion about your friendship. Just say you are focusing on other things right now.

You have future plans with your friend: You might have concert tickets to your favorite band or a trip planned, or a wedding you're going to together. Well, not anymore. Even if you bought the tickets or planned the trip, you have to back out. Tell them something's come up and you can't go, and then give them your ticket. Consider those tickets a loss from the divorce. If it's a wedding or a big event that you still have to go to, then you need to tell them—in a nice way—that you two can't go together. In this case, a little white lie is in order. Maybe you found out that you can't bring a plus-one, or maybe you're bringing someone who you just started dating. Whatever you have to do to get out of the situation, do it.

Your friend tries to make you feel bad: What if they are going through a really hard time? "My friend just got laid off! Their dog just died! They have no other place to live! Have a little compassion. I don't want to make things worse for them!" Your friend may try to win you back with a good, healthy serving of guilt. They may try to woo you with "I'm going through a really terrible time right now, how could you leave me?" They may fake hospital visits, tell you that you are the only person in their life who really cares, call your mother, or make other dramatic overtures. But you must stay solid and get away. Look, if you think this person is going to fall apart without your friendship, then they have bigger problems than losing contact with you. But odds are, they will just find another sucker to take your spot, leaving you free to move into a new relationship, in which you might actually get naked. People like this will literally stop at nothing to get you back in the Friend Zone. Your job is to ignore the pleas and just move forward, no matter whose cat is stuck in a tree.

BUT, BUT, BUT...THAT'S MEAN!

You may think all of this seems cruel. "Why would I treat my friend this way?" Well that's why you're in the Friend Zone to begin with: because you don't think you're allowed to stand up for what you really want. This is about taking back your power and setting your own terms for the relationship. This is about showing your friend that they can't take you for granted anymore and that you won't wait around forever. And this is about stepping away, working on your own stuff and putting yourself first for once. It's not mean. It's what normal people do to get what they want. So try it on for size.

BUT, BUT, BUT...I DON'T WANT TO PLAY GAMES!

"I don't want to play games! I just want to be real and straight-up with people. Games are for liars. I'm an honest person." You are? Really? Do honest people constantly lie to a friend regarding their true feelings for them? Acting like a friend and then secretly smelling their hair as they walk away? Saying "I don't want to play games" is like saying "I don't want to play life." Love does have some element of game playing, no matter how much you wish that weren't true. There's a back-and-forth, there's an exchange of power. You are playing a game; you're just playing it all wrong. So instead of playing the game badly, how about playing to win?

HOW TO SEPARATE WHEN...

You have to see them every day: Avoid your friend without making it obvious. If you normally eat lunch with them, do something else. Eat at your desk and say you've got work to do, or eat with a new group of people. If you normally sit by your friend in a class or meeting, move to a new seat if you can without making it obvious. If you do see each other, keep the conversation really short. You've got somewhere else to be. Say, "Hey, I'm late to a meeting," and then get out of there. Don't make a big deal of avoiding your friend by running away or hiding. Make it as natural as possible.

You have to see them occasionally: If you see your friend periodically for an event or obligation you cannot get out of (company events, church gatherings, volunteer groups), then you need to keep your distance while still being polite. Make a point to keep the contact with them brief. Don't ask any questions, and don't make any future plans.

HOW TO SURVIVE THE SEPARATION

Once you've successfully separated from your friend, read on to find out what to do with all your newfound freedom.

GET A NEW GROUP OF FRIENDS

Now that you are being very good at not initiating any contact with your friend, there's nothing left to do but hole up in your apartment and count the number of dead flies on your windowsill, right? Wrong. Just because you aren't seeing your friend right now doesn't mean you can't see your other friends. Remember them? We aren't trying to turn you into an antisocial, video game–playing hermit. We want you to go outside, go to dinner, take walks, and do whatever it is you do for fun—just not with your friend. Do these things with *other* friends, friends you're not currently in love with. Whatever you do, do *not* talk about your friend. Keep your friend's name off your lips. You'll find that life is so much simpler and easy-breezy with these friends, and who knows? You might even enjoy yourself!

IF YOU HAVE A LOT OF MUTUAL FRIENDS

You can't spend a lot of time with your mutual friends because your friend will be there too. We know how you operate, you and your sneaky ways. You'll plan to hang with those mutual friends in the hope that your friend will be there and then you can torture yourself even more. We're on to you. So, if you two share a lot of friends, consider this your time to separate from that group. Reconnect with old friends, or make some new ones in activities that you don't share with your friend. That way you won't be tempted to ask for updates on your friend. At the very least, you'll expand your circle, and that's never a bad idea. After all, no one on their deathbed has ever said, "I wish I didn't have so many damn friends."

IF YOU'VE SPENT YOUR TIME ONLY HANGING OUT WITH YOUR FRIEND

This is a spectacular time to branch out and meet some new people. No one is bad at making friends, even if you think you are. It might not be your favorite thing to do, but our guess is, if you think you're bad at it, then you haven't really tried. While you're out there, hanging out and having fun with your new friends, guess what you're *not* doing? You're not lying on your bed, obsessing about your friend, wondering why they haven't called, or what they're thinking right now, or if they're out on a date, or when they're going to get out of that terrible relationship they're in. You don't have time for any of that, because you're out in the world, enjoying life with your other friends.

HOW TO MAKE NEW FRIENDS

To make friends, all you have to do is find one thing in common. We bet there are plenty of friends hiding under your nose who you haven't ever noticed before. Look into coed sports leagues, pickup games, classes, theater, gym, and volunteer work. You name a place you've gone in the last month, we'll name at least two new friends you could have made there. Even if you have to go to a meet-up group you found online, go for it. Classes are another great way to meet new people. There's a common goal, even if it's as pedestrian as designing your own website, so you have some-thing to work toward together. You can start by talking to them during the class. Just asking questions about the task at hand is a perfect way to start up a conversation. From there, you can branch out to questions about them, like where they're from or what got them interested in Web design. Then try to take your friendship out of class; suggest going to a movie. And don't let them think you're only interested in making new friends—keep your mind open to other possibilities!

Go for people who are open and receptive toward you. If there's someone who's closed off or not giving you the time of day, move on to the next person. For your purposes right now, you don't need to find a soul-mate-best-friend-for-life. You just need someone to hang out with who's nice and fun and wants to do exciting things. Notice if you're only drawn to people with the same personality type as your friend. If you are, make a choice to befriend someone who's the complete opposite. Drama-free is the way to go here. Give it a try.

GET A FRIEND ZONE BUDDY

Like a workout buddy who keeps you on your toes, you may need a Friend Zone buddy to motivate you through the process. You need someone to call or text when you're jonesin' for your next hit. You can simply ask a trusted friend or family member if you can call or text them every time you want to call or text your friend. It may sound stupid, but it will save you from that late-night phone call or text message that would ruin the Separation. And, believe us, it *will* ruin it.

Take Kim, for example. Kim needed a buddy badly. Her friend was constantly on her mind, and she was used to once-a-minute check-ins with him. She was so tempted one night to text her friend about their favorite band coming to town, but instead she texted her cousin, Aidan. He was always on his phone too, so she knew he'd be around to reply. She asked him to be her go-to Friend Zone buddy. He agreed, telling her that he had been in the Friend Zone before too. She was tempted so regularly that Aidan suggested she actually delete her friend's number from her phone. Aidan said he would save it until the Separation was over. This scared the daylights out of Kim, but she knew she'd be better off without the temptation for a while.

If your Friend Zone buddy wants to get away from their own friend too, all the better. You two can support each other when it seems too hard or you forget why you're doing it. You will also keep each other accountable for sticking to the Separation.

If you feel too foolish asking someone to be your buddy, then simply make them your buddy without telling them. Just make sure it's not a person you are attracted to or who could possibly be attracted to you. Try a family member or same-sex friend. After all, you are not looking for a new "friend." You have enough problems with that as it is.

GET BUSY (GET A LIFE)

Getting a life does not mean "getting a fake life." You really must become unavailable; you can't just pretend. This isn't about updating your online status with "Having a great time on the beach!" when you're really popping a zit with an old earring back and your roommate's magnifying mirror. It's too obvious. Truly getting busy means anyone can tell from a mile away that you've changed. People are on to you when you fake it.

Carla was one of those fakers. She tried to skip this stage by faking a great life. When her friend Jake called, she'd pick up the phone and then get off right away, saying she was "super busy." Jake finally started asking what it was that was taking up all her time. She responded that she had a lot going on. Then Jake got curious. She had hung out with him constantly—now all of a sudden she had all this "stuff" going on? But he never saw her around town; he never talked to anyone who saw her; so *what* was going on? Was she upset with him? Was she trying to make him jealous? *Weird.* He asked her if she was mad and she explained that she was just busy with school and . . . skateboarding. It sounded fake, and she came off like a needy liar. It was all too strange for Jake, and he gave up.

❖ ❖ ❖ ❖ ❖ ❖

"Getting a life" means getting a life. A believable one. And not just for your friend, so they'll believe you when you say you're busy, but for you. Because if you're sitting in your room pretending to be busy while you finish off that second bag of chocolate-covered potato chips, then eventually you will run out of willpower to stay away from your friend. You will cave before the Separation is over, and you won't be able to compete with your friend's real life. Eventually, they'll call and invite you to a real party, and that fake skateboarding class you made up in your head won't be able to keep you from saying yes. Don't put yourself in that position. Go out and do things, and meet new people and experience the world. It's a good thing for you to do anyway. "Okay, I get it, but how do I get a life?" you may ask. We'll show you how in Chapter 7: The Internal Makeover.

HOW LONG SHOULD THE SEPARATION LAST?

You cannot end the Separation until you've gone through your Separation to-do list. In other words, once you're at chapter 8, the Kill, and have done everything in between, you can leave the Separation behind. But not a moment before! You're going to want to end it right away, because a part of you will feel bad and worry that you're being mean, but don't do it. You've got to hold out. If you need some hard-and-fast time guidelines, see the following chart, "Length of Separation." We have broken it down by the type of relationship you had before the Separation, which determines how long the split should last.

LENGTH OF SEPARATION

HOW OFTEN DID YOU SEE EACH OTHER?

All day, every day, by choice:

You guys were attached at the hip. You did everything together.

Every day at work or school:

You saw each other every day, so it's going to take some effort to separate from them.

Once a week, by choice:

You had weekly dates where you hung out and stared longingly at each other. But now, you are going to cut that out.

Once a week, mandatory:

You see each other at a weekly class or at a meeting you can't get out of.

RECOMMENDED LENGTH OF SEPARATION

6 weeks–2 months:

It's going to take a while to get each other out of your systems. Give yourself time.

1 month:

After a month of avoiding them for lunch, they will get the hint.

1 month, at least:

You've got to drive home the point that you aren't going on fake dates anymore. Only real ones.

6 weeks:

Since you have to see each other once a week, it's going to take longer for them to notice anything's going on.

HOW YOUR FRIEND IS GOING TO REACT

If your friend has a pulse, they will have some kind of reaction to all of this. They might get angry and challenge you. They might ask if you are mad at them. They might throw things and cry. They might make you feel guilty. They won't like not being your number one. Your whole relationship has been built on you always saying yes and giving in. They are not used to you disappearing, and they won't like it one bit. They may act like it's a bad thing, but that's good. It means it's working. You want them to notice that some-thing's going on. If they don't notice, then your friendship doesn't mean a lot to them, and that's a problem. That means you may not have had the relationship that you thought you had to begin with. Keep moving forward anyway. The more they react, the bet-ter. Just try to stay cool. Don't match drama for drama. Be the "What ever are you talking about?" person. This will drive them insane, and you want that.

HERE'S WHAT YOU DO

When your friend freaks out, you reassure them and say, "No, this has nothing to do with you. I have a lot going on right now. I'm working on myself. This is about me. This relationship is distract-ing me from changing. I need to get myself together. That's all it is. We're cool." People have respect for someone who is "working on themselves." Those are magic words. If you didn't intrigue them before, you definitely will now. Remember, you told your friend how you feel about them already. Deep down, they know why this is happening, and they probably feel some guilt over their part in it. But that's on them. You just keep doing your own thing.

HERE'S WHAT YOU DON'T DO

Whatever you do, don't make this about your friend. Don't point the finger at them and say, "I need to get away from you," or "I need space from you because I'm so in love with you." In fact, don't use their name or the word *you* at all. Just keep it about yourself and what you need and want out of life. Remember, this person is already having trouble seeing you as someone with wants and needs, so the more you can turn the conversation into what you need, instead of what they're doing to you, the better. Your friend is also trying to figure out if they want to be in a relationship with you, and there's nothing that's going to scare them away more than you coming across as accusatory and angry. That will make them want to head for the hills and never see you again.

WHY YOU'RE DOING THIS ALL THE WAY

The worst thing you could ever do is start the Separation but not finish it. That would show your friend you're even more of a wimp than they already think you are. When you quit before finishing, you are saying, "I have no faith in myself, no self-respect, and no confidence. I'm not strong enough to do this." Remember, gray area doesn't work here. Kind of doing the Separation is not doing the Separation. That just makes it all muddy, and then your friend can't see a clear picture of life without you. The reason you're in the Friend Zone to begin with is because you were vague and took what was handed to you. You can't keep doing that. Follow the Separation through for the length of time that it takes or you won't get the full results.

It may not feel like it, but you're getting your power back. You are taking the lead, and for the first time you are taking charge to get what you really want. This is one of the most difficult steps in getting out of the Friend Zone, but it's good for you. Remember, anyone who's worth your time will be waiting for you when it's over.

Now that you've begun the Separation, you will use this time to take a good hard look at yourself, inside and out. You'll keep what's working for you and get rid of what isn't. It's about removing the easy roadblocks, the ones that you have the power to fix. It's about reaching your full potential, because now you have the time to work on yourself and not worry about your friend. Now let's make over your image.

Dear Wing Girls:

Okay, so I have been doing what you told me and ignoring him for three weeks now. I can tell it is driving him CRAZY! He's calling me all the time and inviting me to places. Yesterday he even said he wanted to make a picnic for me. He never has put this much effort into getting my attention before. It's so tempting to give in and do stuff with him, but I am staying strong! I told him that I just have a ton going on with work and that I have to lie low for a while. I heard from my friend that he is calling around, asking all our mutual friends about me and if I'm dating anyone. I think it's a really good sign. The more he misses me, the happier he'll be to have me back when I stop ignoring him.

CHAPTER 6

The Makeover

Your mom always told you that the inner you is your best part, but no one wants to see your insides when your outsides are screaming, "Get away!" And that's what having stained, dirty, unflattering, unbecoming clothes is saying. Even if you're clean, neat, and take good care of yourself, you may not be exuding an image that's memorable to people. Look at what you're wearing. What does it say about you?

Take Nick, for example. Nick looked like his mother mated with a grizzly bear somewhere around 1978. And yet, he was complaining about his love life. Were the two connected? Yes, of course! Some guys think they are making a "statement" with long beards and greasy hair. We've even heard some guys say their look is supposed to be "ironic." This approach may have worked with Nick's guy friends, but women were not intrigued. If a man is disgusting, he's disgusting, even if it's ironically disgusting. Such was the case with Nick. He thought his look was funny, but the girls weren't laughing. His friend Andrea asked him if he'd find girls with hairy upper lips, gold teeth, or unibrows attractive, even if they told him it was supposed to be an ironic "ghetto Frida Kahlo" thing. He admitted that he wouldn't be into that. He finally decided to cut his hair and shave the nasty beard, and all of a sudden, girls started to check him out.

Maybe you're not as bad as Nick, or maybe you're even worse, but whatever your situation, something is up. We're not only going to figure out what that thing is, we are going to help you become your best self.

WHY A MAKEOVER?

Making over your image will help you reach your potential. You have the ability to move up ten spaces on the "attractive" ladder, but you don't because you're forgetting about all the physical things that draw people to you in the first place. Reaching your potential means using everything you've got and exploiting the best parts of yourself to get what you want. In short: shake what your mama gave you. Yes, you have a great personality, but why can't you also be easy on the eyes? You can! You can have it all, and people won't even hate you for it.

Your friend will see you in a different light. Look, even if you're already the hottest thing since burnt toast, you still need to switch it up so your friend can see you in a way they never have before. You need to show them you've changed, and the best and easiest way to do that is by changing your outsides. You need your friend to look at you and think, "Oh my God, I've never noticed how bright his smile is" or "Wow, those jeans really show off her butt!" It's like when someone gets a haircut and all of a sudden you really look at them, like you're seeing them for the first time. That's how you want your friend to look at you.

You'll become someone your friend is excited to show off to their friends and family. People only feel this way if they themselves are thrilled to be with you. Call us superficial, but a lot of that has to do with looks. If you're hiding behind frizzy bangs, no one wants to bring you home to Mom and Dad, no matter how fun and personable you are.

Your looks may be keeping your friend from seeing what's really amazing about you. Yes, you are intelligent and generous and caring and kind. And those are the things that are truly important in a mate. But maybe your friend can't even see those things because they can't get past your chapped, scabbed lips. That is a roadblock that can easily be removed, so let's take it out and stop clogging up the interstate. Yes, the person you're with is supposed to love you for who you are, warts and all, but if they can't even see the person inside because they're too repelled by your breath, then we need to change that.

You will feel better about yourself. You may be walking around with low self-esteem, and that affects every other part of your life. Fixing your image will help boost your confidence. You may not even realize the effect that feeling bad about your looks has on every aspect of your life. Imagine how it would be to have so much extra room in your brain, room that was previously taken up by all those negative thoughts.

Plus, a makeover will make you seem mysterious. When you come in with a brand-new look, all of a sudden your friend will start wondering what else you're capable of. Your friend will think you are deep and mysterious, with special talents that they can't even fathom. People like surprises. It's exciting. The fact that you didn't consult your friend about this big change will make them wonder what else is going on with you.

HOW TO DO IT

The first step of the Makeover is clearing up any glaring problems that may be getting in the way. After we've fixed those, the second step is figuring out an image that works for you. Ask someone you trust, like a close friend or family member, to give you an honest appraisal. Tell them to put themselves in your friend's shoes and then ask them to be honest and point out anything physical that might keep someone from falling in love with you. Make sure it's a person you are comfortable with, so that you can really hear what they have to say without getting defensive. This is about self-improvement, so it's a good thing if they find a few things that you can fix. Don't go flying off the handle if they point out a split end or two. See "The New & Improved You" checklist on the facing page for some guidelines to help you get started.

WHY GET A NEW IMAGE?

An image refers to your style, which means your clothes, your haircut, and your overall look. Your friend needs to see you in a totally different light, as someone they could be attracted to. One of the most obvious ways to get them to see you differently is to change your style.

We know some of you are thinking, "Clothes, schmothes, they're just rags to put on my body." Wrong. A new style can elevate your perceived status, make you stand out, and can get you attention in a good way. And not only that, what you wear says a lot about who you are. It can say, "Turn away, don't look at me" or it can say, "I'm really interesting. You need to get to know me."

The New & Improved You

SCENT

- Shower regularly. (At least once a day.)
- Wear deodorant. (Make sure it's extra-strength and reapply often.)
- Use a clean-smelling soap that's not too strong.
- Try wearing cologne or perfume. If you're not sure what kind to get, go for the most popular brand. But don't use too much!

SKIN

- If you have acne, get a prescription from your dermatologist.
- If you have dry skin, moisturize at least once a day.
- If you have oily skin, get a good cleanser and use it once a day.

MOUTH

- You should be going to the dentist twice a year for a cleaning and a checkup.
- If you have chapped lips, use lip balm and exfoliate with lip scrub.
- If you have crooked teeth, see an orthodontist to find out about your options.

- If you have any cold sores, get an over-the-counter medication to clear them up (or see your doctor if they're persistent).
- For fresh breath, brush and floss twice a day. Use a tongue scraper and mouthwash.

BODY

- If you feel bad about your body, start working out a few times a week. Get a workout buddy, or hire a trainer. There are a lot of websites and books about eating well to check out too.
- Stand up straight. Just correcting your posture can make a huge difference in how you feel and look.

HANDS

- Make sure your nails are clean and smooth. If you bite your nails or cuticles, try to break the habit.
- Get regular manicures and pedicures. (Guys can get them too.)
- Use hand cream or lotion. If your hands are chapped or dry, you need to get some moisturizer.

NO! I DON'T WANT TO!

Don't want to be with someone who judges a book by its cover? It may sound shallow and superficial, but a lot of times, your style—or lack thereof—is one of the biggest things holding you back from getting what you want: your friend. If you're feeling a lot of resistance to changing up your look, that's just your ego talking. Tell it to shut up and get out of your way.

We're not going to tell you to become someone you're not. But are you really that pair of wide-leg khakis with the huge front pleats? No. You're letting those pants define you, and you're so much cooler than that. Think about what you're wearing right now. What is it saying about you? Does it match who you are on the inside?

Ellie didn't want to change her gothic look. She'd been wearing it for years. She couldn't imagine looking any different. Ellie felt that her look defined her and set her apart from other people. She loved that she looked kind of scary too. Unfortunately, many guys aren't attracted to scary. Ellie was deep in the Friend Zone with Peter, the cute guy who lived next door. Peter thought that Ellie was a good person, and that she shouldn't hide behind that white makeup and those pencil-thin eyebrows. He wasn't scared of her or anything, but he couldn't imagine kissing her with all that stuff on her face.

One day, Peter asked Ellie why she hid behind all the metal studs and black eyeliner. He said he wanted to see the real Ellie, not the gothic version she showed to the world. Ellie was totally taken aback. She had never considered that her look might be contributing to her spot in the Friend Zone. She worried that if she changed her look, she would lose her identity. Who was she if she wasn't dressed in black? What if she wasn't unique and special anymore? But at the same time, she really liked Peter and wanted to show she was capable of growing and changing.

Ellie decided to go for it. She took off her makeup and went back to her natural hair color. She realized she could still be unique without proving it on the outside. Now people were noticing her for her outgoing personality and not her spiky purple boots. Instead of being intimidated and scared of her, they were friendly and smiled at her. Peter treated her differently, too. He was a little flirtier now and he was always hanging around her house, waiting for her to come outside and hang out with him. In the end, she was glad she changed up her look. Not only did it get Ellie out of the Friend Zone, it let her know that it was okay to put herself out there and that she didn't need to hide behind a look that wasn't working for her anymore.

WHAT'S YOUR IMAGE? (FOR GUYS)

Ethan was one of those guys who had been wearing the same outfit since fifth grade. Every day, he came to work in cartoon-character T-shirts, white sneakers, and one of the two pairs of high-waisted jeans that he owned. The other guys at work called them his "mom jeans," but Ethan didn't care. They were comfortable. Besides, he worked in IT, not fashion, so what did it matter? There was one reason Ethan wanted to look his best though, and that was Caroline, the cute office manager. She was smart, funny,and could quote every single episode of *The Simpsons*. She was the embodiment of Ethan's dream woman. Ethan really wanted to ask her out, but he knew that he wasn't really her type. Ethan had seen various guys in leather jackets with expensive haircuts parade in and take her to lunch. He lamented his situation to his roommate, Morgan. She got really excited and clapped her hands and said, "I know exactly what we need to do! We just need to make you look like the kind of guy Caroline would actually date."

At first, Ethan was resistant. He just wasn't the type of guy who cared about clothes. He didn't want to have to wear a costume to get a girl to like him. But Morgan convinced him that right now, he was only running on one cylinder. In other words, he was handicapping himself out of stubbornness. So he let Morgan take him shopping. He bought a few pairs of skinny jeans, even though he had always made fun of guys who wore them. He traded his cartoon tees for plaid button-ups, and after a lot of protesting, he got rid of his orthopedic sneakers and got some black Converse instead.

Finally, Morgan made him go to a salon to get a cool haircut. He whined and asked what was wrong with his cheap barber. Morgan rolled her eyes and pushed him into the trendy salon. But when all was said and done, he looked . . . better. Even Ethan had to admit it. When he looked in the mirror, the guy looking back seemed more confident, more mature. Maybe there was something to this whole makeover thing. Caroline certainly didn't complain. When he came into work Monday morning, she looked at him and said, "What happened to you? You look awesome!" Ethan played it off like it was no big deal, but secretly, was thrilled.

Just like in Ethan's case, you want your friend to do a double-take. You want them to say, "What the heck happened to you? You look so different." The best way to do this is to take a good look at your strengths and figure out how they translate into a style. By the way, your weaknesses can be turned into positives too. How? Well, you know how hipsters aren't known for their 'roid-like muscles? Exactly. So take this quiz to find your best image.

QUIZ FOR GUYS
What's Your Image?

WHAT'S PLAYING ON YOUR IPOD?

a. Top 40 jams, anything I can run along to.

b. My own tracks that I made in my garage last night.

c. My favorite stand-up comic's last show.

d. An old jazz record that I digitally remastered.

WHAT'S YOUR PERFECT SUNDAY AFTERNOON?

a. Going to the shooting range with my friends.

b. Going to a museum to see an obscure photography exhibit.

c. Watching the complete box set of *Family Guy*.

d. Editing the zombie movie I've been working on forever.

WHAT'S UNDER YOUR BED?

a. Lube and a 1970s *Penthouse* magazine.

b. Lube and a sound mixer.

c. Lube and comic books.

d. Lube and old 45 records.

WHAT'S YOUR DRINK OF CHOICE AT A BAR?

a. Whatever gets me drunk.

b. Whatever can be set on fire.

c. Whatever craft beer has the coolest label.

d. I don't really drink—not my thing.

WHAT'S YOUR FAVORITE TV NETWORK?

a. Spike TV.

b. Current TV.

c. Cartoon Network.

d. SyFy.

WHO'S YOUR DREAM GIRL?

a. A girl who looks great in running shorts.

b. A girl who isn't afraid of self-expression.

c. A girl who can make me LOL.

d. A girl who can hold her own in a philosophy debate.

WHAT'S YOUR FAVORITE HANGOUT?

a. A sports bar.

b. Burning Man.

c. Comic-Con.

d. My basement.

HOW DO YOU EAT A REESE'S?

a. All in one bite.

b. Slowly; and I like to make it last.

c. I eat off all the chocolate first and then roll the peanut butter into a ball and throw it in my mouth.

d. I don't—I only eat artisanal chocolate.

WHAT DO YOU DO AT A PARTY?

a. I do a keg stand and get wasted.

b. I glue the beer bottle caps to the bottom of the table.

c. I show everyone the card trick I've been working on.

d. I find a cozy corner and stay there.

WHERE WOULD YOU TAKE A GIRL YOU REALLY LIKED ON A DATE?

a. A hockey game.

b. A poetry slam.

c. A carnival.

d. My favorite coffee shop.

Continued . . .

Results

Mostly As: *Sporty Guy*

YOUR PERSONALITY: You are athletic and like to be outdoors. You are relaxed and laid-back. You get the most pleasure out of socializing with your friends. You are fun to be around, and some people might call you the life of the party.

YOUR NEW LOOK: Your look should be clean and all-American. Think straight out of a Tommy Hilfiger ad. You should go for bright solid colors and crisp lines. Collared shirts and khaki pants or dark jeans should be your staples. Your hair should be low-maintenance and simple. But you don't want to look like a guy on his way to the yacht club, so keep the polo shirts and sweater vests to a minimum.

Mostly Bs: *Artsy Guy*

YOUR PERSONALITY: You are creative, talented, and soulful. You often get lost in your thoughts and can spend hours in the zone with your passion, whether it's playing guitar or drawing. You are intuitive and sensitive. You have a few close friends, and you would rather hang out with them than be in a big crowd. Some people think you are shy at first, but you warm up once you get to know them.

YOUR NEW LOOK: Anything goes, you lucky guy. As an artist, you are expected to experiment. Find your own style and make it work for you. Always play up your best assets. Find a signature piece and make it your own, like a black leather jacket, vintage T-shirts of your favorite bands, or skinny jeans. But remember, you don't want to sport some scary gothic brother-of-the-devil style with your white contacts from Halloween.

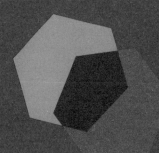

Mostly Cs: *Funny Guy*

YOUR PERSONALITY: You love making people laugh. You're always cracking jokes and goofing around. You love to entertain and have no problem being the center of attention. You enjoy hanging one-on-one with a friend or going out with a big group of people.

YOUR NEW LOOK: You can actually get away with a lot, because you're funny—which means you're not expected to be hunky. You are known for your personality, and that's a good thing. Looking good is like extra credit. But try anyway. Choose a stand-out hairstyle with texture, like curly or spiky. Go for T-shirts with funny sayings on them, like "Tijuana: City of Tomorrow." You can wear shorts, ripped jeans, casual weekend wear all the time and no one will question it, because you've got personality. You can also make people think you've put in a lot of effort by not doing much. Throw a blazer over a V-neck T-shirt if you're going out, and trade in your Vans for some leather dress shoes.

Mostly Ds: *Smart Guy*

YOUR PERSONALITY: You are smart, sensitive, and ambitious. You are very serious when it comes to academics and think you can accomplish anything if you set your mind to it. You have a small group of friends that you are very close to. Socializing is not your biggest strength, but when you discover you have something in common with someone, you find it easy to talk for hours.

YOUR NEW LOOK: It's all about the hair. Since you are a serious person, your hair should be messy and shaggy. Your style should be nostalgic. You can do every time period except the one you are presently in. Old cardigans, skinny jeans, and anything from the '80s or before is a green light to effortless cool for you. Remember that even though you may have a tendency toward more preppy attire, that won't work for you anymore. Experiment a little bit and find a look that stands out from everyone else. Also, throw out those old sneakers. You are not Steve Jobs. Opt for vintage boots instead.

Date Repellent: Advice for Guys

No matter what your new style is, here are a few things to avoid at all costs.

- LONG HAIR (ANYTHING PAST CHIN-LENGTH IS BAD NEWS!)
- CRAZY FACIAL HAIR (IF YOU LOOK LIKE YOU ARE AN EXTRA IN *PIRATES OF THE CARIBBEAN*, YOU NEED TO GRAB A RAZOR)
- ILL-FITTING PANTS (TOO BAGGY OR TOO TIGHT; BOTH SHOULD GO IN THE GARBAGE PILE)
- COMIC BOOK T-SHIRTS (SAVE THOSE FOR COMIC-CON, NOT FOR GETTING OUT OF THE FRIEND ZONE)

WHAT'S YOUR IMAGE? (FOR GIRLS)

Sam was a pretty girl, somewhere underneath those sweatpants and the 49ers T-shirt. Kevin liked Sam, but he saw her as one of the guys, so he never even thought of her as relationship material. Sam was smart, funny, the life of the party. She thought the more everyone else liked her and wanted to be around her, the more Kevin would notice what a great catch she was. Unfortunately, that's not how people work. Sam was finally forcibly given a makeover by her big sister, who was sick of listening to all this "Kevin" business. Sam borrowed one of her sister's dresses, which actually fit her pretty well. Her sister curled her hair and gave her some mascara. The guys all made a big deal about it; some even felt uncomfortable around her now that they saw she was actually a girl. Kevin noticed too. She smelled good. Her hair

What's Your Image?

WHAT'S PLAYING ON YOUR IPOD?

a. Anything hip-hop and upbeat.

b. The latest indie darling.

c. NPR podcasts.

d. Love songs.

WHAT'S YOUR PERFECT SUNDAY AFTERNOON?

a. Playing beach volleyball.

b. Hitting up my favorite flea market.

c. Volunteering at a shelter.

d. Getting my nails done with a friend.

WHAT WAS YOUR FAVORITE SUBJECT IN SCHOOL?

a. PE.

b. Art.

c. Political science.

d. English.

WHAT'S YOUR DRINK OF CHOICE AT A BAR?

a. Light beer.

b. An old-fashioned.

c. I don't drink—I like the green stuff.

d. Pink champagne.

WHAT'S YOUR FAVORITE TV NETWORK?

a. ESPN.

b. HGTV.

c. Discovery Channel.

d. ABC Family.

IF YOU COULD LIVE IN ANY CITY IN THE WORLD, WHERE WOULD YOU LIVE?

a. Sydney, Australia.

b. New York, New York.

c. San Francisco, California.

d. Paris, France.

WHAT DO YOU DO AT A PARTY?

a. A keg stand, my signature move.

b. I always bring my knitting needles.

c. I get into a debate about global warming with some Republican know-it-all.

d. I really don't like going to parties.

WHERE WOULD YOU GO ON A PERFECT DATE?

a. Kayaking and whale watching.

b. A film festival.

c. A drum circle on the beach.

d. A romantic, quiet dinner for two.

Continued...

Results

Mostly As: Sporty Girl

YOUR PERSONALITY: You are outgoing, athletic, and strong. You love being around people. You're kind of a social butterfly. You have no problem talking to anyone. You're always involved in a lot of activities at once. You hate sitting still. You love team sports, and you never shy away from competition.

YOUR NEW LOOK: The girlier, the better for you. Your friend already sees you as one of the guys in a lot of ways. Hair is a big difference between you and him. Make it long and keep it feminine. If your hair is really short, try accessorizing with a headband. If you can get away with it, dye it a lighter color like blonde. Your hair should be beachy and warm.

As much as you want to wear sporty sweats and T-shirts, you have to start wearing dresses. You can still be comfortable, though. Go for long maxi dresses in bright colors and add a few chunky accessories.

Mostly Bs: Artsy Girl

YOUR PERSONALITY: You are artsy and creative. You can while away the hours listening to music or knitting an infinity scarf. You get a lot of pleasure from hanging out with your close friends. It takes you a little while to let your guard down around new people, but once you decide someone is a friend, you are very loyal. With guys, you tend to be a little bit standoffish. This is your shyness coming out as something else. You don't go out of your way to be girly and flirty. You have other things to focus on.

YOUR NEW LOOK: Go for a retro, vintage style with a hint of sexy. Find a look that flatters your figure, like a full skirt over a tighter top. You can mix and match different eras, but make sure you don't go too crazy. Think pinup, not *Brady Bunch*. Also, heels are your friends.

As for hair, go for Bettie Page bangs or any '50s cut. If your style is vintage, your hair should be too. The color should be rich and silky, like dark brown, black, or auburn. Don't be afraid to experiment and switch up your hairstyle. You can wear it curly one day and then put it in an updo the next.

Mostly Cs: *Worldly Girl*

YOUR PERSONALITY: You are passionate, opinionated, and freethinking. You are always thinking about a ton of things at the same time and are involved in a lot of different causes. That doesn't leave a lot of time for socializing and dating, but you tend to make friends in all of your activities. You are a free spirit. You tend to move on quickly from one thing to the next, whether it's projects, friends, or guys you're interested in. It takes a really fascinating person to hold your interest for long.

YOUR NEW LOOK: Since your attitude is really strong, you want your look to be soft and laid-back. Anything feminine and flowy is best for you. You want to go for long dresses and skirts, lacy tops, and bright colors. Feel free to incorporate accessories from your travels—beads from India or tribal bracelets from Ghana. You don't have to hide your passions in your style; incorporate them into your everyday wear; just dress them up a bit.

You want to go for long hair with waves. Severe bobs and dramatic cuts are not for you. If it is short, add some texture with layers and waves.

Mostly Ds: *Sweetheart Girl*

YOUR PERSONALITY: You are sweet, kind, and thoughtful. You put everyone first, especially your friend. You aren't known for your sex appeal. In fact, you tend to hide it. People tend to think of you as younger than you really are because you come across as very innocent. You are very romantic, but you tend to get caught in the fantasies in your head instead of living in the real world. Your friends think of you as dependable and a good listener. You are the first one they go to when they're in trouble.

YOUR NEW LOOK: You need to change up what your friend thinks of you. Something daring and drastic can make them see you in a whole other light. Try dyeing your hair a color you never have before. Or try a dramatic pixie cut or a bob. You want your friend to see you as sexy, so make sure you show off your assets and play up your curves. Stop hiding behind big sweaters and baggy shirts. Wear tight-fitting skirts or dresses with a sweetheart neckline. Go for clothes that show off the best parts of a girl while staying on trend so you can keep that edge.

Date Repellent: Advice for Girls

No matter what your new style is, here are a few things to avoid at all costs.

- DRESSING TOO SLUTTY (HINT AT SEXY, BUT DON'T OVERDO IT)
- CLOTHES THAT ARE TOO BAGGY (IF YOU'RE WEARING YOUR BATHROBE OUTSIDE YOUR LIVING ROOM, YOU NEED TO BURN IT)
- ANYTHING REALLY MASCULINE (STOP BORROWING YOUR BROTHER'S SHIRTS)
- DRY HAIR (IF YOUR HAIR IS REALLY BRITTLE FROM TOO MUCH BLEACHING, GIVE THE DYE JOBS A REST FOR A WHILE)
- TOO MUCH MAKEUP (IF YOU'RE CAKING ON THE MAKEUP BEFORE GOING OUTSIDE, IT'S TIME TO TONE IT DOWN A BIT)

was clean; she had that black stuff on her eyes. She looked like a girl he might actually date.

Just like Sam did, if you want to be seen as a girl, first you have to take a hard look at yourself. You need to examine the following: hairstyle, skin, physique, and clothing. These are some of the things that a guy can't get past, no matter how much he likes you. Think of this step like this: it's about removing the easy roadblocks, the ones that you have the power to fix. Plus, if you have a positive image overhaul, it can only add to your self-esteem. No one ever died from looking too good.

NO EXCUSES

"BUT, BUT, BUT...I'M FINE. I HAVE GREAT STYLE. EVERYONE TELLS ME THAT!"

The whole point is to change, even if your style is passable. Your friend isn't seeing you as a sexual being. That's the problem. The solution? Changing up your look.

"BUT, BUT, BUT...I'M POOR!"

Don't let your wallet stop you from looking your best. That's why there are thrift stores and garage sales. You don't have to mortgage your apartment to look good. Search Craigslist for free haircut opportunities at local beauty schools. You can get free skin care and facials from aesthetician schools. You can watch online videos for just about anything style-related. You can also find workout and fitness videos to help you get in shape on the cheap. Basically, if you want it badly enough, you can make it happen. Money doesn't need to stand in your way; you just have to want it.

"BUT, BUT, BUT...I'M TOO TALL OR I'M TOO SHORT."

Everyone thinks they are too something: fat, short, skinny, or maybe gangly. "My eyeballs are too big. My forehead is too wide," blah, blah, blah. Don't let that hold you back from working it. You can spend your life wishing you could fix something that you can't. Or you can focus on changing the things you can control. Other people don't pay attention to the things you're insecure about unless you give them a reason to. If a tall girl spends her life hunched over, trying to hide the fact that she feels like a giraffe, people will notice that she's standing funny. But otherwise, they wouldn't give it much thought. So put all that effort you've spent trying to change something that you can't into changing the things you actually can.

Now that you're rocking your new look and everyone thinks you're dreamy, it's time to work on what's underneath. As much as your look matters, confidence is just as important. You can't have one without the other. Next, it's time to work on what's inside, so that your friend sees you as the complete package that you are.

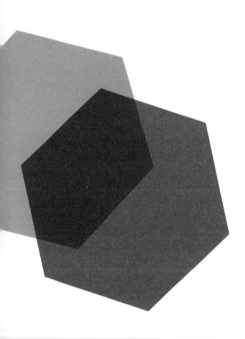

❖❖❖❖❖❖❖

Dear Jet and Star:
I wanted to get out of the Friend Zone so badly, but I really wasn't willing to change anything about myself. I was really overweight for a long time and didn't feel good about myself. Then something clicked and I started going to the gym and working out. I lost a bunch of weight, and all the girls in my class started noticing. More important, my friend noticed too. She has said a couple of times how good I look. I think it's working!

❖❖❖❖❖❖❖

CHAPTER 7

The Internal Makeover

If you asked your friend, "What is it about me? Why don't you love me?" they probably wouldn't be able to tell you. It's not their job to figure it out; it's yours. Maybe it's your lack of confidence. Maybe it's your nonexistent social life, or your Stink City, U.S.A., attitude. Whatever it is, it ends here. Now's the time. If you want this person, you have to make the effort. You can't read this book, drop it on the floor, and then go back to watching reruns of *Boy Meets World* (even though that show is really good), like nothing ever happened.

The Internal Makeover is about creating the best version of you: the sexiest, smartest, most successful, and most confident you. It's about making you a complete person—not waiting for someone else to complete you, but going out and filling in the missing pieces yourself. It's taking what you've got going on and exploiting it to make yourself more attractive to the opposite sex. This is the time to work on *yourself*, figure out what's important to *you*, what *you're* passionate about, and what makes *you* special. But, before we to get to you, we need to look at how you're being perceived. Your friend has given you a label: sibling, parent, therapist, etc. Now you're going to take that label, tear it up into little pieces, and stomp all over it, metaphorically speaking.

HOW TO GET THEM TO SEE YOU DIFFERENTLY

Remember the "How Does Your Friend See You?" chart we did together back in chapter 3? Those were the good old days, weren't they? Well, now we're going to take that role you've been playing and flip it on its head. How do you change the way someone sees you? By acting differently. Whatever your interaction normally is with your friend, you have to force yourself to do the opposite. At first it will be really hard, because you're programmed to do what you've been doing for quite some time. If you're their therapist, you drop everything the moment they're in trouble and need you for something. If you're their parent, you fix things for them because you can't stand to see them in trouble. These roles are fine (occasionally) in a normal friendship, but we all know that's not what's going on here. We're not telling you that now you have to be cruel and stop caring about your friend. But we are saying step back and ask yourself, is your interaction with them helping you reach your goal, which is to ultimately be with them? No, it's not. The role you're playing is not getting you play, and we need to change that.

Obviously you won't be interacting with your friend during the Separation, but you need to start thinking about how you'll change these existing patterns. Remember, the idea with these examples is to get your friend to see you in a different light. You may feel like it's mean, but they need to see that you are 180 degrees from where you were. And you can't jump from one of these roles to the next; that's cheating. It must be the exact oposite of where you currently are. You are not a friend, you are a potential mate. So this is not a guide for how to treat people across the board. It's how to flip the role you're playing and make your friend see you in reverse. When the Separation is over, and you do see your friend again, you'll be better equipped to change the way they perceive you.

Change the Way They See You

PARENT

TYPE OF RELATIONSHIP: You're always fixing things and taking care of them. You can't stand to see them suffer, so you do anything in your power to prevent it.

WHAT HAPPENS	YOUR TYPICAL REACTION (BAD)	OPPOSITE REACTION (GOOD!)
They tell you they're nervous about a job interview.	You go shopping with them for a new outfit, you do a practice interview with them, and you rewrite their resumé.	You tell them good luck and that you want to hear how it goes.
You go out to a party and your friend gets wasted.	You take care of them, you hold their hair up when they get sick, you make excuses for them. Then in the morning you give them a lecture.	You get annoyed and leave them.
Your friend can't pay rent this month.	You get really upset but loan them money and then make them feel bad about it.	You say, "That's too bad. I hope you figure it out soon."

SIBLING

TYPE OF RELATIONSHIP: You are really familiar with each other. You take each other for granted. You tease each other and you're competitive with each other.

WHAT HAPPENS	YOUR TYPICAL REACTION (BAD)	OPPOSITE REACTION (GOOD!)
They fall down in the middle of the street.	You point and laugh.	You help them up and see if they're okay.
They mention someone is hot.	You put the person down or make fun of them.	You agree or brush it off.
They get a haircut.	You make fun of it by calling them Tina Turner.	You say it looks nice.

Continued . . .

▲▲▲▲▲▲▲▲▲▲▲▲▲▲▲▲▲▲▲▲▲
▲▲▲▲▲▲▲▲▲▲▲▲▲▲▲▲▲▲▲▲▲▲▲▲▲

BACKUP BOYFRIEND/GIRLFRIEND
TYPE OF RELATIONSHIP: You act like a real boyfriend and girlfriend, but you aren't sleeping together or calling yourselves a couple.

WHAT HAPPENS	YOUR TYPICAL REACTION (BAD)	OPPOSITE REACTION (GOOD!)
You get invited to a wedding.	You take them, of course.	You ask someone who may be sexually attracted to you.
Your friend needs a ride to the airport.	You give them one and then ask them when you'll be picking them up when they return.	You say you're busy but wish them a safe flight.
Your friend needs to shop for a new winter coat.	You go with them and watch them try on all the coats in the whole store.	You say you hate shopping.

HUMAN PILLOW
TYPE OF RELATIONSHIP: Cuddle buddies, but with no sex. Sex does not exist in this relationship.

WHAT HAPPENS	YOUR TYPICAL REACTION (BAD)	OPPOSITE REACTION (GOOD!)
You stay up late playing Monopoly together.	You stay over and cuddle all night, side by side.	You say you have to go because you need to work out in the morning, and you leave.
You go to the movies.	You snuggle up to them the whole time.	You watch the movie.
They say they are stressed out.	You massage their back and give them a solid rubdown.	You say you hope they feel better, and then you leave them alone so they can figure out their stuff.

SHADOW

TYPE OF RELATIONSHIP: You're always there; they can never miss you.

WHAT HAPPENS	YOUR TYPICAL REACTION (BAD)	OPPOSITE REACTION (GOOD!)
They have a game or event.	You get there early and stay late.	If you go, you show up fashionably late and say you have to be somewhere right after.
They call you and say they're sick.	You show up in five minutes with orange juice and tissues.	You say, "Hope you feel better soon."
They sign up for a new class.	You sign up for it too. How fun!	You let them have the class without you.

THERAPIST

TYPE OF RELATIONSHIP: You are their shoulder to cry on. They call you at 3 A.M. to vent about whatever drama they've been having. You never get to talk about your own stuff; it's all about them.

WHAT HAPPENS	YOUR TYPICAL REACTION (BAD)	OPPOSITE REACTION (GOOD!)
They tell you they got in a fight with their friend.	You stay up all night asking them questions, making them explain and figuring out what to do. You actually feel anxious or angry, as if it's happening to you.	You say, "Awww, that sucks. Sorry."
Their pet dies.	You are so upset, it feels like your own pet died. You listen to them for hours. You do everything for them. You cry with them!	You say, "That's terrible. I'm sorry to hear that."

GETTING A LIFE

A major part of the Internal Makeover is getting a life. Part of what makes someone attractive is that they have a lot going on. They have passions, hobbies, things that excite them beyond any "friendship." Now that you're in the Separation phase, you have the time you need to explore what makes you happy, aside from your friend. Here's how getting a life will make you more attractive.

Luke was really into Danielle—embarrassingly into her. He dreamed about her and made up songs about her beautiful brown hair. She couldn't see him as anything but her shadow. They worked together on a political campaign, and when it ended, Luke spent all his time thinking up excuses to see her. He bought tickets to bands she was into, even though he was not a fan of electronica music. He scoured the Portland events calendar looking for stuff he thought she would want to do, like art fairs and comedy festivals. And then one day Danielle asked him, "Luke, what do you like to do in your free time?" He realized so much of his time had been devoted to doing what he thought Danielle would like to do that he didn't really know anymore. He made it a point to figure out the answer to this question.

One rainy Sunday, he made a list of the things he liked to do, the things he'd been neglecting in his quest to hang out with Danielle. He wrote: "Run, fix bikes, and play drums." He found a local running club that met on Tuesday nights and joined up with them. He started helping out at a bike shop on the weekends. He liked the people who worked there, and hung out with them at a nearby brewery after they got off. He also started playing the drums for a new band that some friends of his from high school started up. With all his new activities, he didn't have time to pore over the events calendar and highlight the things that Danielle might want to do. But then a funny thing happened. She started calling him and inviting him to do things with her. For the first time in their friendship, he wasn't bending over backward to get them to hang out together. He may not have realized it at the time, but this was his first step out of the Friend Zone.

GETTING A LIFE MEANS...

Saying no. As we said before, one of the most difficult parts of the Separation is saying no to your friend when they invite you to do something. If you are actually busy doing your own thing, then turning down an invitation is a lot easier.

Having a full life. Your friend needs to know they are not the only thing in your life. Up until now your friend has felt like your life begins and ends with them. They feel a lot of pressure knowing that they mean so much to you. Your friend felt like they didn't have to try at all, because you'd already put them on a pedestal. And your friend would walk all over you, because they knew they could. If suddenly your friend sees that you've got a life outside of your friendship with them, they'll realize they need to make an effort to become a part of it.

Having a passion. Having a passion makes people want to be around you. If you're passionate about something, whether it's music, or art, or football, or hat-making, it gets people excited. People like seeing someone who is really good at what they're passionate about. That is sexy. And believe us, being seen as sexy is going to help your cause. A lot.

Not always being around. People want you more when you're not there. Just as absence makes the heart grow fonder, when you are not always in your friend's line of sight, they think about you more. They will actually take the time to wonder what you're up to, which is something you haven't given them the space to do before. By being busy doing your thing and living your life, you will spark your friend's curiosity, and they'll get to feel for once what it's like to *want* to hang out with you, to miss you even.

HOW TO GET A LIFE

This is the fun part, because it's all about you. It's about what you like to do, what you're drawn to, and what interests you. Here are some ways to get started.

Take classes: Classes are great because they're a fun, low-pressure way to get out of your comfort zone and try something new. Plus, they're a good way to meet people and make new friends. Community colleges have classes for all kinds of subjects: Photoshop, salsa dancing, movie editing, photography, etc. You can also look up local classes for stand-up comedy, painting, knitting, whatever floats your boat. Or you can get active and take yoga or spin class, or trampolining for adults. Yes, that exists!

Connect with a new group of friends: The minute you branch out and start hanging out with some new people, you will find all sorts of invitations coming your way for whatever they're up to: movies, parties, bowling, what have you. The best way to get invited out with those friends is to take the lead and invite them to something that you're organizing. It doesn't have to be a big hullabaloo. You can just say, "Hey, I was thinking of making some pizza and watching *The Godfather* trilogy. Why don't you guys come over?" Done and done!

Get a Hobby

SPORTY	MUSIC	ARTSY	INTELLECTUAL
Coed sports teams	Join a band	Painting	Book club
Swim club	Open-mic night	Craft groups	Writers' group
Runners' group	Song circle	Co-op art galleries	Museum docent
Rock climbing	Record collecting	Photography classes	Political meet-up
Gym classes	Local shows	Knitting circle	Chess club

Get involved: A great way to get busy is to volunteer. Not only are you getting yourself out of the house, but you're also doing good for your community, and people will think you are selfless and caring. Oh, and added bonus: you might even meet some cuties while you're at it, which won't hurt your cause at all. Plus, by volunteering, you will put things in perspective. Yes, you may be stuck in the Friend Zone, but at least you're not sleeping on a park bench. There are volunteer opportunities everywhere: homeless shelters, the Humane Society, wildlife centers, the Big Brothers Big Sisters program, American Red Cross, Habitat for Humanity, libraries, etc.

Say yes, even if you don't want to: Have you ever seen the movie *Yes Man*, with Jim Carrey? Well, that's what you're about to become. Or a Yes Woman, as the case may be. You are going to say yes to whatever opportunity or event comes your way, even if you don't want to. You never know what will be waiting for you there: new people, new opportunities, and new memories to be made.

Try something different: Change up your usual routine. If you drive by a park every day and think, "One day, I'm going to go play basketball over there," then today is your day to do that. If you normally go right home after work this time, invite a coworker out to happy hour with you. Just switching up your routine will make you remember that there is a big world out there.

Join a team: Sign up for an intramural softball team, or join a community ultimate Frisbee league. Joining a team will introduce you to new people, give you a set schedule for games and practices, and get you moving around too. That's a whole lot of benefits in one. And don't forget about the fans who come to the games. Stick around after you hit the game-winning home run. Some adoring fans might want to shake your hand, or buy you a drink—and some of them might even be cute!

Take yourself on a date: How cute, right? You don't have to buy yourself flowers or make out with yourself on your doorstep, but take yourself out and do something fun. Go to a museum by yourself, or go to a concert or an outdoor festival. Take yourself out to dinner. We bet you'll find you are really good company.

WHAT MAKES YOU HOT?

Conner was friends with a really cute girl from the dorms named Melissa. She was very nice and sweet, and a lot of other guys thought she was hot too. Conner could tell Melissa liked him, but there was something missing with her, something that kept her in the Friend Zone. He really didn't know what it was. Then he met Tori. Tori was not as cute as Melissa and the guys didn't make a big deal about her. But Conner thought Tori was cool and was dying to get to know her better. Every time he was around her, he got excited and pictured asking her out.

Tori was extremely intelligent and was on the traveling debate team. She was always getting really mad about animal rights issues, and she marched in front of the science building to protest their treatment of research animals. One time, she even yelled at Conner for eating a hamburger and smacked it out of his hands. She apologized later but made him promise not to eat another one in front of her again. Conner didn't ever really care about that kind of stuff, but he thought it was so cool that Tori did. Melissa didn't really do anything except go to school and parties. Sometimes, Tori was so into her cause that when he would see her in the hall, she would barely pay attention to him and then run off when she saw another member of her animal rights group.

Girls always paid a lot of attention to Conner, so it was strange when Tori didn't. When Conner saw Melissa and asked her where she was headed, she always said "Nowhere" and looked at him longingly. Then they went to lunch, where they stared at each other for twenty minutes while Melissa asked him questions. Meanwhile, he'd usually see Tori out of the corner of his eye trying to get someone to sign a petition to stop testing cosmetics on animals. Melissa was prettier, but she paled in comparison to Tori. Melissa was in the Friend Zone because she never had a passion. She didn't have something in her life that was more important than Conner.

Every attractive person has something they care about more than getting a boyfriend or girlfriend. That's a big part of what makes them attractive. Have you ever seen the ugly rock star guys with the supermodel girlfriends? Well, the rock stars have a passion, and it's greater than their need to find a mate. The trick here is not to become something just because you think that's what your friend wants. If Melissa sees Conner's interest in Tori and her passion for animal rights, that doesn't mean she needs to go rescue a pregnant cat. And if Conner loves rock climbing, that doesn't mean Melissa has to start swinging from mountaintops either. The idea is to find something you're good at or that you enjoy. Don't choose something just because you think your friend would like it. That would totally defeat the purpose. So find something that you absolutely love and do it.

WHAT YOU'RE DOING WITH YOUR LIFE

Amber was going through what her friends called a "slump." A two-year slump. She had taken a leave of absence from a PhD program because she just wasn't motivated in her classes. She felt like researching fourteenth-century literature was pointless. How was being able to deconstruct Chaucer's *Canterbury Tales* going to help her in the real world? She'd been working at a local café full time ever since. It was a stupid job, but it paid the rent, and it was only temporary. The slump was no big deal; she would crawl out of it eventually. But the trouble was that Amber's crush on Ben wasn't going anywhere. Ben had just started law school. He was moving up in the world, and Amber was still slumpin' it. How was she ever going to win him over while slinging lattes in a puke-red apron, when he was hobnobbing with the preppy law school women of New England?

What Amber and anyone else in this situation needs to do is take a good hard look at what's going on. She needs to ask herself: Am I living up to my potential? Am I using my talents to the best of my abilities? Most important: Would I date me? Would I be proud to bring someone like me home to meet my family and friends? Amber would easily answer no to all of these questions. The thing is, she's not a loser. She is smart and capable and interesting. But she's not motivated. Amber's stuck in a rut and she's accepting it as just one of those things that will eventually pass. Sure, it's making her miserable and not very fun to be around, but who can blame her?

Well, *we* blame Amber for not fighting harder. She knows she's not living her best life. And Ben knows it too. It's hard to "get it up," so to speak, for someone who's not fighting for themselves. It's just plain unattractive. If you're in a situation like Amber's, you need to light that fire under yourself and do something about it. Don't give your friend any more excuses to write you off as an unfit partner. Show your friend that you're motivated and that you can apply yourself. It all starts with you. If you believe these things about yourself, then other people will believe them too. Don't let your slump become an excuse for all the things you're not allowing yourself to get. You deserve better, so go for it!

Even if you're not in a slump, but you know you're not totally applying yourself at work or school, then look at what you can do to improve. Settling for a ho-hum existence is not attractive. If you don't think you're worthy of achieving your dreams, then what makes you think you can be with the person of your dreams?

ARE YOU A SLOBBY SLOB?
As you embark on making yourself over from the inside, it's a good time to look at the message you're sending out to the world. Are you broadcasting, "I take pride in myself" or does your message

say, "I am a hot mess. Stay far away"? Take Bobby, for example. He had a lot going for him. He was smart and funny; had a ton of friends and a killer fast pitch. But his car was disgusting. It was a big joke among his friends that no one wanted to carpool with him. When a friend entered his car, they couldn't see the floor beyond piles of soda cans, chip bags, and gym socks. How was Bobby ever supposed to pick up a girl for a date in a moving trash can?

The thing is, he probably wouldn't, because once she got a look at the passenger seat, she'd be running for the hills. Take a good hard look at the areas of your life where the mess is. If it's your home, your car, or your desk, now is the time to do something about it. No matter how awesome you are, those piles of trash are going to keep people from seeing anything else. They are going to think that every area in your life is just as disgusting and chaotic. While you're going through the Separation, you have a perfect opportunity to turn it around and show that you're not the slob that your friend thinks you are.

DATING OTHER PEOPLE
Another big part of the Separation is dating other people. Even though you might not feel quite like dating other people right now, you have to for a few reasons. One, it will make your friend jealous. And believe us, nothing is a better aphrodisiac than a little jealousy. Most of us don't realize we want something until the chance of getting that thing is threatened. By going out with other people, your friend will suddenly realize that your heart doesn't live and breathe for just them. They may have to step up their game a little.

Andrew was head over heels in love with Chelsea. He was always inviting her out: to watch him DJ, to go to concerts, etc. All Andrew wanted was for Chelsea to be his girl, and she knew it. But she didn't see him that way. He didn't want to do the whole separation bit at first; in fact, he fought it for a long time, but he finally realized it was his only shot. He stopped calling her, he hung out with his other friends, and he picked up more DJing gigs so he wouldn't be tempted to hang out with her on the weekends. But he really didn't like the "talking to other girls" part. He didn't want to talk to other girls. He was interested in Chelsea, and he knew she was the only girl for him. But then he found out she'd started seeing someone. So he called up other girls he knew. He went out with them to concerts and parties, and you know what? He even enjoyed himself.

One of those girls developed a little crush on Andrew, and she told him so. He told her things were kind of complicated at the moment, and she said she understood. In the meantime, Chelsea caught wind of all this. She started asking around to find out who Andrew was dating. Everyone told him she was jealous.

Toward the end of the Separation, Andrew showed up at a party with three of his new "girlfriends." Chelsea was there too. She came up to him and asked him to dance with her. She teased him about his new "girlfriend." Clearly, she was jealous. Andrew is now out of the Friend Zone and dating Chelsea. A huge turning point in their relationship was when he started dating other girls. Do you know why? We do:

It made her jealous. Yes, it's the oldest trick in the book, but a little jealousy goes a long way. You don't know how bad you want that red velvet cupcake until the woman in front of you in line snatches it up and then all of a sudden you're ready to knife her for it. When Chelsea saw another girl interested in her Andrew, she suddenly realized what he meant to her. And she realized that she didn't want to lose him to someone else, especially to a cheesy girl with stringy extensions.

She saw him as a sexual person. Remember that moment when you saw your younger sibling with a boyfriend or girlfriend for the first time and you thought, "Eww, they'll have sex one day"? It never occurred to you before, because you don't look at them as a sexual person. Well, that's how Chelsea had been looking at Andrew for so long: as asexual. But then she saw that another girl was into him, and it suddenly struck her like a bolt of lightning: "Somebody thinks Andrew is sexy!" And then, "Wait, Andrew *is* sexy!"

Dating other girls boosted his confidence. You know how dogs can smell fear? Well, humans can smell desperation. And there's an inverse relationship between how attractive someone is and their level of desperation. It puts a grime on even the coolest of people. But now that Andrew knew he had other girls interested in him, he had no reason to be desperate with Chelsea, because he knew that if she rejected him, he could get another girl. And that made him feel more confident. And confidence equals sexiness.

HOW TO DATE OTHER PEOPLE
You don't have to get really serious with anyone, or update your relationship status. We're talking about dinner and a movie; you don't even have to get dessert. You don't need to sleep with them or be their date to weddings; you just need to sit across from them over dinner or coffee and smile and laugh when they say something marginally funny. You won't have to feel the pressure of asking someone you like out in these situations, because you don't even know if you like them. Frankly, it doesn't matter. This is for

you, not them, so you won't have to worry about the sting of rejection. If you ask them out and they say they can't, no love lost.

Here's how to do it:

Approach strangers. A good way to meet new people is to literally meet new people. Go up to someone you don't know and start a conversation with them. It can be someone at work you don't normally talk to, a person in your yoga class who smiles at you every now and then, or your cute neighbor who accidentally takes your mail sometimes. All you have to do is smile, introduce yourself, and ask them a few questions. If you hit it off, you should trade phone numbers and set a time to go out.

Meet people through friends. Your friends are a gold mine of potential dates for you. If you haven't taken advantage of this yet, then where have you been? Let them know you are open to being set up. A lot of your friends will love to do this; they will be thrilled that they're getting to play matchmaker. But let them know that you're not looking for anything serious at the moment, just someone to have fun with, so that they won't be hurt if you don't wind up getting married to whomever they find for you.

Try online dating. Dating on the Internet is an easy way to feel really popular with pretty minimal effort. You sign up, fill out your profile, say something witty about yourself in the description, mention your love for animals, put up a picture of yourself doing something adventurous and sexy like bungee jumping, and then *boom*! Fifteen interested candidates in your inbox. You don't have to date all of them, but you'll find that even messaging them gives you a different outlook. You suddenly realize that there are a ton

Rules for Dating Other People

- DON'T GET TOO INVOLVED WITH SOMEONE YOU'RE NOT THAT INTO.
- ALWAYS USE PROTECTION IF YOU'RE GOING ALL THE WAY.
- BE HONEST WITH THEM. TELL THEM YOU'RE NOT LOOKING FOR ANYTHING SERIOUS.
- DATE AROUND. IT'S OKAY TO GO OUT WITH A FEW DIFFERENT PEOPLE FOR THE TIME BEING.

of people walking this earth, people who are looking for the exact same thing you are, and when you zoom out of your current Friend Zone situation, you see that even if you and your friend don't wind up together in the end, your life is far from hopeless. There are plenty of fish in the sea, or at least on the Internet.

Ask people out. This is your chance to ask people out just for the sake of going out. There's nothing huge at stake, so you might as well try it on for size. Be that guy for once, the guy who just asks out every girl who strikes his fancy. Or the girl who says yes to a guy she normally wouldn't. You never know, you might enjoy your-self. It's much better than sitting by the phone, waiting for your friend to call.

SELF-ESTEEM
Not everyone is born with high self-esteem. Sometimes you have to build it up over time. Having self-esteem makes you attractive

on the outside. The more of it you have, the more other people will want to be around you. It takes effort ("No! Not effort again!") to get to the point where you genuinely like yourself. The trick is to fake it till you make it. Here are some tips to help you build up your self-esteem:

Don't talk badly about yourself. There is nothing worse than listening to someone put themselves down. It's really unattractive and makes the other person notice all of those things and dislike those parts of you too.

Do esteem-worthy acts. When you do something good for someone else, you feel good. Helping an old lady across the street not only helps her, but it makes you feel better about yourself and your worth, and that, in turn, makes you more attractive. Who knew that old lady was helping you get laid?

Make a list of everything you're proud of. Making a list of all your accomplishments or even just things you like about yourself and reading it when you feel blue is a great way to build up your self-esteem.

Smile. Yes, it sounds stupid but it's true. Smiling when you feel like beating yourself up really helps you get out of your own head. It tricks your mind into thinking you're happy.

Give compliments. If you want a world where you get compliments, start giving them. Putting a smile on someone else's face makes you feel better about yourself.

Stand up straight. The right posture and stance can get you everywhere. Standing up straight tells the world you have pride in yourself.

ATTITUDE

Have you checked your attitude lately? How's it looking? No one wants to sleep with the sad sack in the corner moaning about the economy. Is that you? Here's the thing: if you aren't happy at least half the time, you are in serious trouble. It's hard to get people to want to be around you if you are full of poison. You'll need to make some changes.

In any situation, do you always look at the negative side of things? If so, your perspective needs to shift to the positive. Even if you really hate a certain state of affairs, you need to consciously think about its good aspects and try to focus your attention there. Smile even if it's painful for you. The more you do this, the better it will be for everyone around you.

SEX APPEAL

Believe it or not, the lack of sex appeal is a huge reason why people wind up in the Friend Zone. Sex appeal is that X factor that excites people around you. When you've got it, people find you more interesting. It has nothing to do with looks. Sex appeal is basically charm, charisma, and attitude.

The first step in assessing your sex appeal is to figure out how your friend sees you. Do they think of you as asexual or too overtly sexual? If they see you as asexual, then they think you have no sex appeal. If they see you as overly sexual, then they're seeing too much sex appeal.

SEX APPEAL: HOW TO GET IT

Sex appeal is one of those things, like confidence or a sense of humor, that seems to come naturally. But the good news is, that's

Are You Overly Sexual or Asexual?

DO YOU EVER TALK ABOUT SEX WITH YOUR FRIEND?

a. All the time.

b. Sometimes, but rarely.

c. Never. We would both be grossed out.

WHEN YOU SEE SOMEONE OF THE OPPOSITE SEX WHO'S ATTRACTIVE, WHAT DO YOU SAY?

a. "I'd like to do some damage on that!" Then you high-five someone nearby.

b. "That is the cutest butt I've ever seen."

c. Nothing.

WHAT IS SEXY ABOUT YOU?

a. Everything. (But especially my private parts.)

b. My smile.

c. Me, sexy? I'm going to need some time to think about that.

DESCRIBE YOUR SENSE OF HUMOR.

a. The dirtier the better. I like making my friends uncomfortable.

b. I like telling funny stories about things that happen in my life.

c. Self-deprecating. My friends love to laugh at me.

RESULTS

Mostly As: Overtly Sexual

Tone it down. Your message is getting across loud and clear. You don't have to let everyone know you're sexy by broadcasting it across all channels. But there's so much sexiness going on with you that people are starting to think you're all talk. They're wondering if you are yelling about it from the rooftops because you're trying to distract from the fact that you have no idea what you are talking about. Next time you're about to turn a normal conversation about fruit into something dirty, don't. Take a deep breath and hold that thought. Everyone will start to think how mature and subtly sexy you are.

Mostly Bs: Sexual

You're about right; you just need a tune-up. You talk about sex every now and then, but you know when it's inappropriate. Your friends know they can joke with you about blow jobs without making you cry. So you just need to fine-tune your sex appeal.

Mostly Cs: Asexual

You'll need to turn it up. You are polite, sweet, and a little shy. You never talk about sex because you don't want to offend anyone. You respect the opposite sex and know that there's more to them than their lower half. We love and appreciate that about you. But you are still a human being: a human being with needs and wants and desires, just like everyone else. Admitting to that every now and then is a good thing. It will remind your friend that you think about sex just like everyone else. Don't bend over backward to avoid talking about sex or kissing or whatever's in between. We know you're blushing just thinking about it. But go on, dip your toe in that dirty water.

not totally true. If you're someone who doesn't naturally have sex appeal coursing through your veins, don't worry, because you can change that. Here's how to get some sexy swagger:

Have confidence. Confidence is the biggest determinant of sex appeal. People who believe in themselves and think they are great have loads of sex appeal. Why? Because confidence is sexy. So work at it. Practice believing in yourself and your actions. Don't second-guess yourself all the time, especially not out loud. The more you practice it, the more you'll believe it.

Work what you got. People with sex appeal also know what they're working with, and they use it to their advantage. These people have turned what others see as flaws into assets. Everything about you—good and bad—makes you who you are. So take the things that make you unique and work 'em.

Do what makes you happy. Sex appeal comes from being happy, and the easiest way to find happiness is to do what makes you feel that way. Think about the times you're at your happiest. What are you doing? Are you painting, horseback riding, gardening, listening to music, shopping, playing sports, cleaning out your closet, etc? Whatever it is that makes you smile, do more of that.

Watch your body language. Do people with sex appeal spend their life hunched over in a little ball, hiding from the world? Or do they walk tall and proud and stick their chests out and say "Hello, world!"? Look at how you stand when you are in public. A lot of times, it's little things like posture that make a huge difference in how people see you. Stand up straight, uncross your arms, and puff out your chest. You will feel better just by making those slight adjustments. Think about what your body language is saying to people around you. Is it saying, "I'm open. Come talk to me. I am friendly"? Or is it saying, "Get the hell away"?

Be positive. People are attracted to positive people. It's no great secret of the universe. People want to be around you if you're happy and have a good attitude.

Be mysterious. People equate mystery with sex appeal. They are intrigued by someone they can't quite pin down. You are not an open book. You don't have to explain every single one of your actions all the time. Do you feel like hanging with a new crowd today, or switching up your look, just for the hell of it? Well, do it, and don't explain yourself to any of your friends, and suddenly people will think you're mysterious.

Jeremy was what all his friends would call a sweet guy. He had been in Lisa's Friend Zone for what seemed like forever. (Really, it had been about two years.) On paper, Jeremy made a perfect boyfriend. He had a good job, an active social life; he was smart, funny, cute, nice, and he loved pets. His mom couldn't understand why he never had a girlfriend, with all his qualifications. And honestly, neither could Jeremy.

The problem with Jeremy was not on paper. It was in real life. It was the way he couldn't talk about sex without turning it into a joke. He once asked a girl if he could kiss her and then said, "Just kidding—you have mouth herpes." Any time the subject of kissing or sex or intimacy came up, he retreated by laughing about it. It was fine with his friends, because that's what they did. But when he did that stuff with Lisa, she thought that he was immature. Even though he was cute, she couldn't imagine hooking up with him. In fact, she couldn't imagine him hooking up with anyone. She bet he would just burst out laughing the minute he got to touch a breast.

It's the way Jeremy deals with the things that make him uncomfortable that's robbing him of his well-deserved sex appeal. Since he's treating the subject of sex like a five-year-old would, he comes off as having the sex appeal of a five-year-old, which is unfortunate for a grown man. This is the main thing keeping him in the Friend Zone with Lisa. The sooner he grows up and treats the topic of sex like an adult would, the closer he'll be to getting out.

WHY GIRLS LOVE ASSHOLES/WHY GUYS LOVE BITCHES

Ever wonder why you are stuck in the Friend Zone while the biggest jerk in town gets all the play? It's because they have certain qualities that keep them from getting stuck in the Friend Zone. We're not saying you need to be cruel to get your friend to like you. But you do need to steal some of the jerk's attributes for your own. Following is a diagram that shows the good qualities that you can take from both assholes and bitches.

An asshole or bitch doesn't care what other people think of them. They live their own life and do what they want to do. They don't wait for approval from anyone. They don't build their life around another person; they wouldn't dream of it. People love this. They are drawn to it. This is why when you find out your friend is dating someone else, it's always someone you would deem a jerk. This makes you mad, because you'll never be anything but a nice person. You can't help it—you're just nice! But that's not the problem. The problem is that you don't have a passion, or you care too much about what other people think, or you are codependent: issues that assholes and bitches have absolutely no problem with. If your

ASSHOLES
- Manipulative
- Misogynistic
- Rough
- Inconsiderate
- Emotionally unavailable

BOTH
- Confident
- Independent
- Do their own thing
- Don't care what other people think
- Passionate about something

BITCHES
- Mean
- Selfish
- Short-tempered
- Bossy
- Spoiled
- Want everything their way

friend is always talking about an asshole or a bitch who they like or are dating, that should be an indication that you are doing something wrong, not that they are attracted to the wrong people.

In the end, you want to be a nice person with the good qualities of an asshole or a bitch. You want to be a "nasshole" or a "nitch." You want to have confidence and not be dead-focused on someone else. And you want to say no whenever you feel like it. You have to learn that "No" is a complete sentence, and you don't have to justify it to anyone. You are going to be that type of person, or at least try to be.

Will was a "nice guy." He was constantly talking about it—that's how we knew he was so nice. He used it as an excuse for everything. Someone got a raise at work who didn't deserve it when Will did? Well, that's because Will was nice and the boss only liked the assholes. Someone got the last ticket to a concert by cutting in line? Same thing. Being nice was such an awful existence, it made him totally depressed. The world doesn't reward nice. So when it came to Hannah, the coolest girl he knew, he was doomed. She had jerks falling all over her. And it seemed like the guys she dated were all jerks too, not abusive jerks, just guys who thought they were all that. This really annoyed him. He thought, "If I bragged about my life like him and wasn't subtle about my feelings, then I would have her too. But I won't change who I am for someone else—I'm a nice guy, and someday someone will appreciate it."

Not only is the nice-guy excuse totally untrue, it's also a crutch. Guess what? You can be nice and stand up for yourself. You can jump-start your neighbor's car *and* say you have to leave by five when your boss is giving you a guilt trip. You don't have to be a "nice guy" or an "asshole"; you can just be a human being with a backbone.

Girls do it too. They say, "Well, I will never be a bitch, so I guess I'll just have to find a guy who appreciates it when I do his laundry without asking. I guess I'll just have to find a guy who appreciates it when I bring him lunch at work." Those things are reserved for when you are actually in a relationship with someone. In the beginning it seems too intimate too fast, and that scares people away.

Ava had a really hard time getting out of the Friend Zone with Mason. She couldn't quite grasp the concept that men really did like "bitches." She thought that if she was a good person and always went with the flow, Mason would grow to appreciate her. All the other girls he dated gave him a hard time and were so annoying, and he complained about them constantly. But once he broke up with one bitch, he always moved right along to the next one. He would complain that they took too long to get ready, that they were totally selfish, that they only did what they wanted to do, and that they spent all their time hanging out with girlfriends. He would tell Ava how bossy they were and how they always fought him on things. Ava didn't get it. She thought, "Mason is just going through a phase. One day he'll see what he's been missing. I'm always here for him and always available when he wants to hang out. I always go to baseball games with him when none of those other girls would be caught dead there. I'm cool and so nice. I'm just so nice!"

Oh no, not the N-word again. Look, if nice and passive got you laid, then you wouldn't be reading this book and you certainly wouldn't be in the Friend Zone. Guys like girls who do their own thing. Puppies are cute when they wait around and respond to your every move, but it doesn't work that way with guys. So remember, take the things that work for a bitch and use them to your advantage.

IF NONE OF THIS IS ENOUGH

Maybe your problem goes beyond your friend. Maybe you need help with something beyond your control, and it's getting in the way of your having a good relationship with anyone. If that's the case, there are plenty of options, and just like with your Friend Zone situation, you don't need to settle for less. You don't have to do it by yourself. There are therapists and support groups you can find. If you are getting fall-down drunk every night and wondering why your friend is so turned off, it could be time to look into that.

Or if you are so moody you make your family members cry or run away every time you walk in a room, maybe it's time to go see a doctor. If you have major abandonment issues, so bad that you put pressure on your friendships, maybe you should talk it out with someone. Whatever it is, if it's not helping you reach your goals, then it's time, especially during the Internal Makeover, to get some real help.

There are very few people on this planet who are lucky enough to get to push the pause button and take the time they need to work on themselves. Consider yourself one of the really lucky ones, because you get to take a time-out from your friendship, take a good hard look at yourself, and give some attention to the things that need it.

No matter what happens with your friend, this will serve you well in the future, because you're working on improvement. That's not just for this friend of yours but for all the people you have yet to meet. Who you are right now is temporary. You're not the same person you were five years ago, and five years from now, you'll have changed a lot too. But for right now, this whole Internal Makeover is about becoming the very best version of yourself.

The next step is revealing your new and improved self to your friend and asking them out at the same time. You cannot move on until you've actually done the steps required for the Makeover and Internal Makeover. If you don't fully do them and act too soon, it's never going to work. There is no rush on this. It's better to take too much time than not enough. Make sure you really devote yourself to the process. Even if you have to read this chapter a couple of times to make sure it really sinks in, that's okay. We'll be waiting for you when you're ready.

Hi Wing Girls:

I was in love with this guy for three years, and he just wanted to be friends. I know it probably would have gone on like that forever, so I had to do something about it. I've been avoiding him for about a month. At first it was hard, but it's actually been really good for me. I realized what a clingy stalker I was being, calling him all the time, showing up to his place. Now I've found all these other things that I've forgotten I was into. It's made being with him not seem like such a life-or-death situation. I seriously used to obsess over him all the time. I'm so glad I'm not doing that anymore!

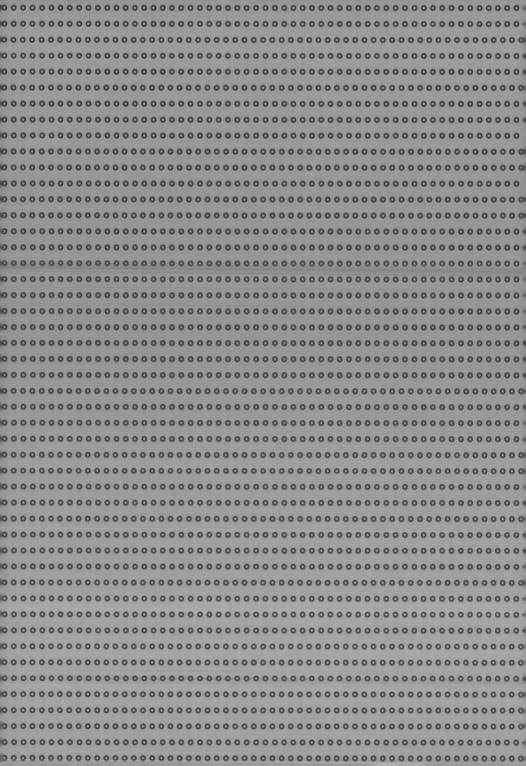

Part Three

. . . .

MAKING YOUR MOVE

CHAPTER 8

The Kill

You've done all the hard work: you've made over your image, you've worked on yourself, you've suffered through the Separation. Now it's time to go in for the Kill, which means you will ask your friend out on a date. A real date. The Kill is the moment of truth, when you will see if they still see you as a friend, or if there's room for more. This is what you've been waiting for. It's do or die.

You need to accomplish a few things during the Kill: drive home the fact that you have changed, let your friend know that you two are speaking again, and make it clear that you are asking them out on a date. This is when you end the Separation—by asking your friend out. Just like we've told you before, the very worst thing that can happen is your friend saying no. Even if they do, at least you'll know for sure and then you can move on with your life. But let's bank on a yes, because after all, who wouldn't say yes to you? We're going to tell you exactly what to say, how to act, and how to read your friend's response to make the whole process as pain-less as possible.

IF THEY WANT ANSWERS

Your friend might want to get into the drama of the Separation now that you're finally talking to them again. They will grill you for answers, they will pick fights and try in the most dramatic way possible to get you to tell them why, oh, why you did this to them. "How could you? You abandoned me! You left me all alone!" They might even try to put the drama on you. They may say, "Why are you so dramatic? Why couldn't you just be my friend?" Your response, as usual, will be to keep it light, say you've been extremely busy, and that you've been working on yourself. You could even say you were going through something very personal but now things are fine. Remember, when you address them, do it in an unemotional, vague, and easy-going way. Your friend wants a monumental reason why you would abandon them, they want the drama, and, most important, they want to know you still need them in that embarrassing way you used to. Do not give your friend this satisfaction. This is the turning point where they see they really can't walk all over you, you won't be waiting around forever, and you have a life outside of your previous obsession with them. So you must hold your ground here. Don't give them what they want. If you do, you may move all the way back to the beginning, and all your work would be for nothing.

SETTING

Setting the mood is the most important part of the Kill. A couple of things to keep in mind: If at all possible, do it at night. Everyone is more romantic at night. Try for the nighttime, or at the very least, dusk. Also, during the Kill, try to be in a somewhat romantic setting away from other people. If you are in front of the Taco Shack and your friends are all running around fake-farting from the beans, you might as well call it a night. As much as you can, try to control your environment. If there is a pretty tree or a park bench or even a quiet spot at the bar, edge that way instead of hitting your friend up in front of the bathroom. You've come this far; why not aim to make the Kill romantic?

HOW TO DO IT (FOR GUYS)

If you're a guy, here's what you do, step by step:

Tom was the kind of guy who was so shy he could barely look at himself in the mirror for fear of an awkward conversation. The Separation part was fine for him. It was summer and he was home for the break anyway. One day toward the end of the Separation, he saw an old picture of him with Maya, his friend. He couldn't believe he used to spend every single day of his life with her. He'd grown so much since last June, not just in muscle mass, but in everything else too. He took up surfing and made a bunch of new buddies. He had dated three different girls—well, two and a half; one winced when he kissed her, so she didn't officially count. He couldn't even imagine seeing Maya again on campus, but he knew just where to find her. She would be at the SAE frat party that first week of school.

Tom prepared a script and knew that to ask her out he had to get there after her first beer but before her fifth. When he walked up to her, she was shocked. She couldn't believe how different he looked. She just kept saying, "Oh my God." He'd brought some friends along, so if it ended badly they could still have a fun night. Maya said she'd really missed him and asked what he had been doing all summer and why he couldn't hang out with her. Tom used his script and told her he was really busy with surfing and the beach cleanup. She was stunned by the way he looked and acted. Then Tom said he'd been thinking about it and wanted to take her out, and that an all-female AC/DC cover band was playing on campus next week and he had two tickets. Maya smiled and said yes. Tom said, "Great," and then he walked away. Even though it took everything he had inside him to do it, he was so glad that he had.

Script for Guys

YOU: Hey, (name).

HER: Hey, (name).

YOU: It's been forever. It's good to see you (or talk to you, if you see her a lot).

HER: Yeah, you too. I thought you'd dropped off the planet.

YOU: Thanks. Sorry I've been so busy. A lot's been going on.

HER: That's okay *or* I know, what the hell? *(Drama drama drama.)*

YOU: Well, I gotta get to _____, but I'd really like to take you out. What are you doing this weekend?

HER: Not much *or* I have something. *(If she says she has plans, ask her when she is free.)*

YOU: Cool. Pick you up at eight?

HER: Okay, see you then!

The key is to not make the conversation about anything but setting up the date. Anything else will muddy your chances. Don't get into it, don't talk for more than five minutes; she needs to want to see you, so give her that chance. Get in, make a plan, and get out. Leave her to wonder what just happened.

IF YOU SEE HER EVERY DAY

If you see your friend every day, you know you will have a moment where you can walk up to her and ask her out. You know when she's going to class or when she's on her coffee break at work, so there is no awkward phone call in your future. You can do it in person, where she is much more likely to say yes. When you see her, you can smile and act as though nothing has happened between you. Just say that you've been so swamped and got really into [fill in the blank]. If she tries to get into the reasons why, don't go there. Just get to the point where you ask her out on a date. If she says no or tries to get out of it, say, "The offer's on the table, so just let me know." And then walk away.

IF YOU ONLY SEE HER ONCE IN A WHILE

Asking someone out in the flesh is much better than any other method. So, if you only see them every once in a while, make it a point to be somewhere you know your friend will be. If she always hangs out at the same dive bar every Tuesday, then guess where you're going? You'll be there with some friends of yours, and you'll be prepared to go in for the Kill. Start with a simple "Hey, how are you?" And then go straight for the jugular.

IF YOU HARDLY EVER SEE HER

If you really have no chance of seeing her, then on this occasion, and this occasion only, you are permitted to make a phone call. If you call her and she doesn't pick up, leave a message simply saying: "Hey, it's _____. Give me a call back when you can." Make sure your tone is happy so she doesn't think someone died. If she does pick up, then ask her on a date as quickly as possible. The phone call can go on no longer than five minutes. You're in, and then you're out.

HOW YOU SHOULD LOOK THAT DAY

This is the day when the style you've cultivated during your make-over comes into play. Make sure you wear something that makes you feel confident and sexy. Also, you need to be clean and smelling good. Pick the outfit that makes you feel your best, but if you are planning on running into her at a football game, don't wear a suit and tie.

HOW TO DO IT (FOR GIRLS)

Girls, don't think you are getting away with doing nothing. You've got work to do too!

Lindsay had done everything right during the Separation. She had stopped sitting next to Sean during work meetings. If they ran into each other afterward, she would give a quick smile and then say she had to go and make up some excuse. She had gone out with a few guys from her softball team, just for drinks or coffee, nothing serious, but she heard from a friend that Sean wanted to know who she was dating. She was proud of herself for really giving the Separation a shot.

Lindsay knew that Sean was going to be at a coworker's birthday party, so she got dressed up. She didn't want to be too fancy—after all, they were going to a bar that had a mechanical bull—but she put in some effort. She curled her hair and wore a top that she knew made her boobs look good.

When she showed up, she went right over to Sean. She smiled at him and gave him a hug. He seemed surprised to see her, or surprised she was talking to him, she couldn't tell which. He offered to buy her a drink and she let him, even though usually she would give him money, or say, "I got the next round." She asked about him and what had been going on since the last time they hung out, which was a while ago. Sean made a few jokes about all her new boyfriends, but she just laughed it off, saying that she was trying to expand her horizons. He rolled his eyes. Lindsay did her best to flirt. She leaned into him, she laughed at the jokes he made, and she teased him. And then toward the end of the night, Sean turned to her and asked, "Hey, what are you doing on Saturday?" Lindsay thought about it and said, "No plans yet." He asked if she wanted to go try the new sushi place that had just opened up. She said, "Sure," and he replied he'd call her later to make plans.

Driving home that night, Lindsay thought something had been different about the way they interacted. It hadn't been all jokes and high fives like usual. She realized the problem this whole time had been her. It had been the way she acted with him. For the first time ever, she showed him a different side of her, and it worked.

IF YOU SEE HIM EVERY DAY

If you have classes together, or work together, or carpool, or do something where you have to see each other regularly, then your job is to pick a day to end the Separation. Mark it on your calendar, so there's no going back. On this day, you're going to definitively show him that things are different. You've got to flash some signals to let him know that you're no longer pretending that he doesn't exist. You're going to dress up a little more than usual. You've already done your makeover, so he will notice there's something different about you. Smile when you see him, and initiate contact. Don't wait for him to do it, because you've been avoiding

Script for Girls

YOU: Hey, (name).

HIM: Hey, (name).

YOU: It's been forever. How are you?

HIM: Pretty good. About the same. Where've you been all this time?

YOU: Oh, I've been really busy with _____ (name something: community theater, work, remodeling). *(Remember, easy-breezy!)*

HIM: That's cool. Glad you're back now.

YOU: Yeah, I've missed you.

HIM: I've missed you too. Maybe we should go out this weekend and catch up.

YOU: That would be great. Just not Friday, because I have plans. But maybe Saturday? *(Don't be COMPLETELY available; you have a life, remember?)*

HIM: Saturday's good. I'll text you to figure out where to go.

YOU: Okay, great! I've got to get to _____. Good seeing you...(name). *(Guys love it when you say their name!)*

him for weeks, so he's not going to expect you to actually open your mouth and talk to him. Don't be surprised if he looks a little shocked at first.

It's important that you act easy-breezy about the whole thing. "Hey, how've you been? What's up?" Be casual. You don't need to hang a sign around your neck that says, "OKAY, SEPARATION OVER, NOW ASK ME OUT." However, that is the point of the Kill: to get him to ask you out! You need to go on a date together, a real live date where he picks you up, and then you have awkward pauses over dinner. That kind of date.

Act interested in him, be available, and be flirty. You know how to do it: smile, laugh, tease him, and ask him questions. At this point, give him a window to ask you out. You can hint, as in, "What are you doing this weekend?" or "I need to hear what you've been up to, we should hang out," but let him do the asking. That's how you'll know he's interested. Give him time to ask you, be patient, and lay the groundwork for the Kill to happen.

IF YOU ONLY SEE HIM ONCE IN A WHILE

If you don't see him every day, then the Separation might have been a little easier, because you haven't had to work very hard to avoid him. But that makes this part a little harder. You have to give some clear signs that the Separation is over. Pick a day when you know you will see each other again. Maybe you know you'll see him at temple this Friday, or at the tournament that his rugby team is playing next week. Whatever it is, decide that the next time you see each other will be the end of the Separation. When you know you will run into him, doll it up a little bit, wear perfume, and then show him by your actions that you are happy to see him. From here on, follow the steps we laid out previously.

IF YOU HARDLY EVER SEE HIM

If you and your friend live in different cities, or if you only hang out every once in a blue moon, then you have to try the hardest of all to end the Separation. If you do nothing, you'll spend the rest of eternity stuck in the Separation, and that won't help you much. Try to run into him naturally. We're not telling you to stalk him, but if you "happen" to see on Facebook that he's got tickets to a stand-up comedy show then maybe you should get yourself a ticket, and let fate do the rest.

If you try and try but you know that fate's not going to meet you halfway, then pick up the phone and call him. If you get his voice mail, leave a message that says, "Hey, call me when you can." If he answers, then do the same things you would have done if you were seeing him in person: act happy to talk to him, be flirty, laugh, and ask him questions. You can make it like you're just calling him to catch up.

On this phone call, leave the door open for him to make future plans with you. If he lives out of town, ask, "When are you coming back here for a visit?" If he lives close by but you just don't hang out much, then say, "I've got to go, but it would be great to hang out and catch up." If he has a pulse and is even mildly interested, he should get the hint and ask you out.

HOW YOU SHOULD LOOK

Take the style that you've been working on during your makeover and rock it. A dress never hurt anyone. Show off your best features. Make sure you smell good and look your best. Leave your lips kissable and your hair soft. If you never wear heels, this is a good time to do so.

LAST RESORT

Ladies, we've all been in the position where the guy we're after just doesn't get the hint. Maybe he had a partial lobotomy and can no longer interpret subtext, maybe he's secretly saving himself for his wrestling partner, or maybe he is paralyzingly shy. Whatever the reason, you have led the goddamn horse to water. You have stood there and patiently whispered, "Drink, please drink, FOR THE LOVE OF SAINT CHRISTOPHER, TAKE A FREAKING SIP!" And he hasn't done a thing. In this case, we're not going to tell you to spend your days sprawled out on the silk divan in your dressing gown, waiting for him to call. This isn't *Pride and Prejudice*, and he's no Mr. Darcy. While we are advocates of letting the man do the asking, there are times when a girl has to take matters into her own hands. If we're speaking to you right now, then listen up. You need to go ahead and ask him out. It's the only way to know where you stand. If you do this, first make sure that you have done all the outlined steps: flirt, act interested, drop hints, show you're available, etc. If you have done everything and still come up empty-calendared, then you are going to do the asking. You should make it nonchalant, like, "Hey, I was going to get fondue with a friend tonight, but they're sick; do you want to go instead?" or even "*Paranormal Eight* comes out next week and no one is brave enough to go with me. Are you up for it?" Don't make it a big deal, like, "This is a real date, so you better run for your life." Act as if you have lots of other people to ask and you're just going down the list.

WHY WE WANT THE GUY TO ASK

When it comes to going out with a guy, you shouldn't have to do all the work. A lot of girls in the Friend Zone feel that they have to mastermind every situation, that they have to control everything. If you have to ask him out, then that is just the beginning of the work you'll have to do during that relationship. It means you'll be planning the dates, you'll be figuring out the next time you're going to see each other and where you're going to go, and he will learn very early on that he doesn't have to lift a finger, because you are driving the bus. Women are really good at driving the bus (and men are good at riding along), but in a relationship, you want a partnership where your guy meets you halfway. Also, people tend to want something more if they have to work hard for it, which is where the thrill of the chase comes from. If you make it too easy for a guy, he might take you for granted. Normally, we would say, "Do whatever you need to do." But you are in the Friend Zone for a reason, and that might be because you're not letting him do any of the work.

WHAT IF THEY SAY NO? (FOR GUYS AND GIRLS)

"But what if they say no?" First you need to ask yourself if you did everything in your power to get them to say yes. Did you actually do the Separation? Did you date someone else and make them jealous? Can you honestly say that you followed each step to the best of your ability? If not, go back to chapter 5 and give it another go. There's nothing wrong with that. Sometimes you need a practice round before you really know what you're doing.

If you're sure you did everything you could and gave it 100 percent, then take that no for what it is: a flat-out no. Consider yourself lucky. You don't want to be with someone so narrow-minded they wouldn't even try to give it a whirl. This person can't even fathom dating you, so much so that they won't even give you an evening of their time. Do you really want to be with such a person? Your answer better be "HELL NO!" But if it's not, and you feel they were being reluctant for some other reason, you can say, "Well, if you want to go out sometime, let me know." Leave the ball in your friend's court and seriously let go of it for now. The most important thing is that now you have your solid reply and can move on. You know that they don't want to date you, so now you can find someone who actually does.

At this point, you need some time away from your friend. You need to really get them out of your system. It will take falling in love with someone else for you to be able to have a normal, platonic friendship with this person. Know that you have to give it some time. We know that right now it feels like a loss, but at least you have clarity and can move on with your life.

Whatever you do, don't go back to being friends with them right away. This will just cause more heartache, because you haven't given yourself time to heal emotionally. You need to separate yourself from your friend until you are fully and truly over them. In the coming chapters, you'll learn how to keep yourself out of the Friend Zone in any future relationships, so you never have to go through this again.

THEIR RESPONSE: HOW TO INTERPRET IT

Unfortunately, not everyone will give you a straight-up yes or no. Girls will usually say something other than what they really mean under the guise of not wanting to hurt your feelings. And guys may say yes, but their body language may tell a different story. The following "What Guys Do" and "What Girls Say" charts give some possible responses and what they mean.

What Guys Do

WHAT HE DOES	WHAT IT MEANS	GOOD SIGN?
He hesitates.	I don't think this is a good idea, but I don't want to hurt your feelings.	No
He makes you ask him.	I'm a coward *or* I'm not into you.	TBD
He doesn't seem excited about going out.	I'd rather be doing something else.	No
He says yes but then flakes.	I wanted to say no, but didn't know how.	No
He says yes right away.	I wanted to ask but was afraid of rejection.	Yes
He says he's busy but suggests another day.	I really am busy that day, but I want to go out with you.	Yes
He suggests his friends come along.	I want to keep you as a friend.	No

What Girls Say

WHAT SHE SAYS	WHAT SHE MEANS	TRY AGAIN?
I'm busy right now.	No chance in hell.	No
Let me check my schedule.	I need to weigh the repercussions of dating you before I make my decision.	Yes
I'm busy tomorrow night, but I'm free next weekend.	I'm playing hard to get.	Yes
I'm dating someone.	I'm not interested.	No
I might have something going on.	I have to check with my friends to see what they say about you.	Yes
I have a big project due the next day. Can I let you know the day of?	If something better comes up, I'm canceling on you.	Yes
I'm not into guys anymore.	No freaking way.	No
I'm babysitting . . . for the next two weeks.	I don't want to go out, but I want to let you down easy.	No
I'm going out for dinner, but you can come over after.	I don't want to be seen in public with you, but I'm curious about us.	Yes
I'm helping my girlfriend pack, but call me and we'll see.	I'm planning on blowing you off, but I might change my mind.	Yes
I don't eat dinner.	Either I'm anorexic or I have no interest in you.	No
I'm focusing on myself right now.	It's not you, it's me. No, actually, it's you.	No
I just went through a really messy breakup.	I can't think about dating someone else right now.	Yes

WHAT'S NEXT?

Now that you've got your date lined up, that's literally half the battle. You've done the hard work; you've ripped that Band-Aid off. It's time to reap your reward. You get to be one-on-one with the person you've been dying for. In the next chapter, we're going to talk about the fun part: the Date. We'll make sure you're good and prepared for it before we send you on your way. But for now, take a deep breath and pat yourself on the back. Think about where you were when you started this process. Think how much you've changed and all the things you've learned. We know a lot of this has been scary, and maybe you had to get out of your comfort zone a few times, but wasn't it worth it? A few months ago, would you ever have dreamed that you'd be going on a real date with the friend you've been fantasizing about forever? No, didn't think so. You are well on your way to leaving the Friend Zone for good, and never looking back!

❖❖❖❖❖❖❖❖

WG:
I had been in love with this girl, who
always saw me as a friend, for the last
two years. In the past, whenever I thought
about asking her out, I literally felt like
throwing up. But I knew that it was either
do it or stay in the Friend Zone forever,
and that would be way worse. Yesterday,
I finally asked her on a date. It felt so
good to be honest and know that either
way, no matter what she said, I wouldn't
die. Bonus was when she said yes.

❖❖❖❖❖❖❖❖

CHAPTER 9

The Date

You have waited a very long time for this night. If you took all the minutes you've spent fantasizing about the Date and spread them in front of you, you could probably get to China. That's a whole lot of buildup. Now you get to claim your prize. This is the fun part. Dates are fun! And you like fun, right?

Now you actually get to go out with your friend, whom you've been crushing on for what feels like forever. You get to sit next to them in the car, you get to steal sidelong glances out of the corner of your eye, you get to think about kissing them good night, and you get to call your friends later and tell them how it went, down to every tiny detail.

Obviously, this is a big moment for you. This date could change everything from here on out. No pressure. You've got some things to do before you can get to the magical goodnight kiss. But don't worry, we're going to tell you exactly what you need to do to make this date unforgettable—not "the day I split my pants in public" unforgettable, but "the best night of my life" unforgettable.

The most important task in front of you is this: to show them this is a date and not a hang-out. You might think they already know this, but don't be too sure. You guys are friends. You've hung out before, probably one-on-one. You've gone to movies, just the two of you; you've sat across from each other at dinner; you've gone through the motions of a real date even when it wasn't. So how are you going to make this different? How are you going to show them beyond the shadow of a doubt that this is a real honest-to-god date and you are not messing around anymore? We'll show you.

PREP FOR THE DATE

You have to make yourself look like someone your friend would want to be seen with in public. That's just the way it is.

ON THE OUTSIDE (FOR GUYS)

You've spent all this time getting ready for your date. Is this really the day you want to skip brushing your teeth? On the contrary, this is the day you want your breath to be so fresh it could melt the hair off the guy sitting in front of you on the subway. You want to smell so good, people stop you on the street to ask what on earth you're wearing, and mean it in a good way. You want to prepare for the possibility of some tonsil hockey, so you want your lips to be soft and kissable. For style, a general rule is to look better than you normally do, but don't dress up so much that you make your friend feel uncomfortable and you look too desperate.

Guys, don't use the Date as an opportunity to show off the vintage *Charlie's Angels* T-shirt you bought off eBay last year. The Date is when you need to look good, in a hot and sexy way, because remember, she doesn't see you like that. She sees you as the guy she uses to prop her up when she's feeling bad about herself, or the buddy she calls when the guy she likes doesn't call her back. You've been working on your style anyway; just take it up a notch.

Wear something you would feel comfortable wearing running into anyone you know, but not something you'd wear to a backyard BBQ. You probably want to ask your sister or a female friend to help you pick something. Remember, your friend needs to see you in a whole new light, and what you used to wear isn't going to cut it. Styles may vary, but make sure your clothes are clean and ironed and that you smell like a *man*. You don't want her to confuse your cologne for her Bath & Body Works spray or her dad's feral cat musk. For facial hair, get it trimmed by a professional if necessary. Get a haircut if needed, but do it a few days if not a week before the date, so you don't look like a third-grader on the first day of school. Remember to aim to look like the guys she picks up the gossip magazines to gawk at, or at least get as close to that as you can.

ON THE OUTSIDE (FOR GIRLS)

We know this is going to sound dangerously close to "Bitch, get in the kitchen," but it wouldn't kill you to wear a dress. There, we said it. Now we can cringe our way through the rest of this. Look, somewhere down the line, this guy stopped seeing you as female. Maybe he didn't exactly see you as male, but somewhere in between the two: somewhere deep in the Friend Zone. In order to get you out of there, you need to become like the girls he checks out while you are holding his shopping bags and trailing behind him. Those girls most likely wear dresses and do their hair and makeup. If you ask any guy what his favorite look is on a girl, he'll say "sundress." True, it is no longer 1991, but he will still say it. Now, maybe your friend is a goth who could think of nothing worse, but you'll still see his head turn when a feminine girl in a dress walks by.

Now that we've established you're wearing a dress, the next step is asking a friend who has great style (guy or girl, maybe even a couple) what you should wear. Either go buy something new or give them a tour of your closet. Also, wear something you are comfortable in. If you are pulling and scratching and going crazy, that's not a good look either, and you might as well show up in your hole-in-the-crotch sweats. Wear something that makes you feel sexy and pretty so he'll think of you that way too. Make sure you have your hair down and touchable. As much as we love a great beehive updo, tonight is not the night. Tonight is the night he'll hopefully want to touch your hair, so go for the softest hair you can personally have. Slapping a guy's hand away from your head is okay on date four, not date one.

Now, makeup is a tricky one. Guys all say that girls look better without makeup, but we know that's not always true. What they mean is, "Don't have junk all over your eyes and don't wear lipstick because then we can't kiss you, but have incredibly long lashes and look really glowy, fresh, and dewy, and we'll pretend that means you have nothing on at all." So go for a more natural look, but make sure you play up the cheeks, the eyes, and the skin. If you need to, ask a friend to do your makeup or go to a makeup counter. In general, just pump it up for the date.

ON THE INSIDE
Remember that as much as you think the Date is the culmination of your adult life, it's really not. We aren't saying to phone it in, but you don't want to completely freak yourself out. Being slightly nervous is natural, but you don't want to come across as someone who spent last night in a meth lab. You need to at least pretend

to have serenity about it all. Look, at this point, you are ready for this. You've done all the prep work, and now you get to suit up and show up. It's like studying really hard for an exam. When you walk in to take it, you know you've done all you can, and you're ready to breeze through it. That's how you should feel on the Date. You've been doing all the work, so you'll know what to do in any given situation. You're prepped and ready to go. Plus, you are sexy, interesting, passionate, and an all-around great catch. Who wouldn't want to be with you tonight? You've got it goin' on!

WHERE'S THE DATE?

Close your eyes and picture your idea of a perfect date. Got it? Okay, now open them so you can read this. Get ready, because we're going to read your mind: it's during the day…someplace really crowded and loud…with really bright lighting…and a lot of screaming kids nearby. Are we right?

A good date is all about the setting. It's got to be at night, no matter what every MTV dating show does. People are just not as lovey-dovey in the cold light of day. If it's not dark out, don't even bother, and if you live in the North Pole where it stays light for twenty-four hours straight sometimes, then date in the winter.

Now let's talk about the lighting. You don't have to sit in a room filled with candles, but dim lighting is best. People are more self-conscious in bright light. If your friend can see every blemish on your face, then you can see theirs too, and that's not going to make your friend want to rub up against you. When you're thinking about where you want to go, consider the lighting. That's why movie theaters are good choices, or concerts, or dimly lit restaurants. We all look better when the lights are low.

Now think about how many people are going to be around. If you're surrounded by strangers, you two are going to feel weird talking about anything intimate. That's why amusement parks are a bad idea for a first date: because you're going to spend all your time waiting in line with a family of six loud kids in front of you. Choose a place where you and your date can have some privacy. But you don't want dead silence, either. There's nothing worse than hearing crickets while your soul shrivels and dies. Choose someplace with background music or a little chatter.

Another thing you want to think about is the romance factor. You want it to be subtle and not lay it on too thick. If you two are at a restaurant surrounded by couples who are getting engaged left and right, and the violin quartet doesn't leave your table long enough for you to have a conversation, that's going to get pretty awkward. Your job is to bring the romance. Let the place just hint at it. Now that all that's taken care of, what are you actually going to do on this date?

The best date is a two-parter. Part one is an activity (such as ice skating, a movie, a comedy show, a concert, a sporting event) followed by some quiet time (such as a quick dinner, coffee, drinks). That way, you get out a lot of the nerves and the awkwardness right at the beginning while you focus on whatever activity you're doing. You're not staring at each other across a table trying to think of what to talk about; you're involved in something else. Then, when the activity is done, you can sit across from each other, but you'll actually have something to talk about. You can recount the fun you just had, or talk about the movie you just saw, or make fun of the guy behind you who kept snorting every time he laughed. It's not dinner and a movie; it's a movie and dinner. Just make sure the second part is not a six-course meal where you are sitting with a dripping candle for four hours. Make it short and sweet and leave your friend wanting more. This is not your anniversary dinner; this is a hot, quick appetizer for all the fun you'll have when you're officially together.

Daniel felt like he'd been waiting to take Suki on a date his entire life. Really, he had only known her for a year. She was his friend's stepsister. But from the minute he'd laid eyes on her, he couldn't stop thinking about going out with her. He had done everything right. He had gotten through the Separation like a champ. He had made her miss him. When he asked her out, she seemed genuinely excited about going out with him.

Daniel took a poll of his friends and family to decide where to take her on the Date. At first he was going to take her out to dinner, but the consensus was that eating dinner was too boring. He needed to do something different, to wow her. He knew Suki was really into animals. She had three cats and was even training to be a veterinarian. So he decided to take her to the zoo.

He picked her up at noon and didn't tell her where they were going. When they got there, they got in line to buy the tickets. It was crowded that day, and hot too. They waited in line at the ticket booth for almost an hour. The baby behind them threw a tantrum because her monkey balloon popped. He tried to keep the conversation going while they were in line, but he felt like he was running out of things to say.

When they finally got inside, Suki took one look at the giraffe behind the fence and burst into tears. Daniel didn't know what to do. When he asked her what was wrong, Suki mumbled that she hated to think about these animals that belonged in jungles but were now locked in cages. That's when Daniel realized he'd made a horrible mistake. This place was the furthest from romantic he could have gotten. He had this vision of the two of them kissing on the bridge that overlooked the chimpanzee den. But when they got up there, it smelled like poop. And the chimps were all watching them with their big monkey smiles. It made him uncomfortable. They left after an hour. Daniel asked her if he could take her out the next week to make up for it. Suki said she'd think about it.

Daniel took Suki to the zoo in an attempt to please her, but he didn't think about what was would set the Date up for success. The Date is not a "Gee, where would we go on my friend's birthday after we've been dating for two years?" It's more like, "What would be a great date for anyone?" Daniel overthought her interests and didn't think enough about setting the mood. He took her out during the day, which is never a good idea. Also, there's no better birth control than screaming kids, or kids in general. And any activity where you're going to spend half your day waiting in line isn't going to set the mood for anything but a nap.

HOW TO MAKE IT FEEL LIKE A REAL DATE

You need to make your friend feel like there has been a big shift between you two. In other words, it needs to feel like a *date* between two people who like each other; there's no more pretending. That part is over. The Date should look like it's straight out of the *Lady and the Tramp* spaghetti scene. Read on to find out how.

Ideas for Your Date

Draw a line from an activity in part one to an activity in part two that goes along with it.

PART ONE	PART TWO
Comedy show	Drinks at the bar next door
Concert	Coffee shop
Karaoke	Pizza place
Roller-skating	Diner
Scary movie	Ice cream parlor
Baseball game	Walk on the beach

FOR GIRLS

As horrible as it may sound, for the Date, let him take the driver's seat. Let him open doors for you; let him pick you up and pick the movie. Part of the "courtship" process, even though that word gives us the heebie-jeebies, is letting him at least think he's taking the lead. Make him feel like this date was his idea, even if it wasn't.

Cheyenne was one of those girls who punched guys in the arm and burped the alphabet. She didn't understand the whole girly-girl thing. On the other hand, she sure did like Steve. He was such a dreamboat, it made her want to scream and jump up and down like in those old black-and-white videos of girls at Beatles concerts. Steve didn't see her as a girl, obviously, and called her his "kid brother" as a joke. After a long Separation and quite a stunning makeover, Steve finally asked Cheyenne on a date. The problem was, she didn't know how to interact with him without that "pants-ing each other in the middle of an all-you-can-eat shrimp buffet" shtick. And unfortunately, she thought that post-makeover she could still behave the same way. She thought losing twenty pounds put her in the clear. After a night of kicking his ass at paintball and out-guzzling him at the brewery, she could tell it wasn't going so well. Steve looked kinda weirded out when she started staring at him and puckering her lips in the car.

Cheyenne didn't win Steve over because she failed to recognize how important it is to set the scene. The truth is, the Date is when you should clearly define things on your terms, and if you fail to do that, then the shift from friend to more than a friend can't happen. You have to be aware of your interaction with your friend and send a clear message that this is a real date.

FOR GUYS

Guys, the opposite goes for you. You pick her up, try to make the decisions, and take the lead. Make her feel like you aren't her asexual robot-friend. Show her she is a woman and you'd love to treat her as one.

A side note for guys, though: don't try too hard, don't bring pres-ents, don't be overly complimentary, and don't be too romantic. There is a fine line between being attentive and being a sweating, bulgy-eyed creeper who cuts off pieces of her hair and makes a memory box with them.

Tyler really liked Marika. They were coworkers at a coffee shop in San Francisco. Marika was constantly complaining about all the jerks she dated. She wondered where all the romantic guys had gone. Tyler listened to her and thought that he would surprise her for their date with a sunset cruise across the bay, a bed full of rose petals, and a locket with his picture inside. Instead of impressing Marika, he totally freaked her out. She was used to complete jerks, so this was too much, too soon. She didn't feel that she'd earned that quite yet and said that she would expect this kind of treatment a year from now with an engagement ring at the end. She said she wanted romance, but what she really meant was that she wanted Tyler to look her in the eye when he was talking to her and pay for the movie tickets.

There is a definite limit to how far you should go, even romantically, on the first date. Tyler blew it by taking things way too far. Don't let this be you.

IS THIS A HANG-OUT OR A DATE?

This may be a question your friend is asking themselves. See the following "Hang-Out or Date?" chart to make sure you do all the things in the Date column and avoid anything on the Hang-Out one.

Hang-Out or Date?

	HANG-OUT	DATE
How do you get there?	Meet there	You pick her up
What do you order?	Coffee	Dinner and wine
What do you talk about?	Her terrible current relationship	Your future kids
What's after dinner?	Nothing	Dessert
Physical contact?	No way	Yes, yes, and yes!

WHAT TO TALK ABOUT

We don't need to tell you how to talk to your friend. You guys have been friends for long enough that you know how to talk to each other. But since this is a date, there are a few guidelines you should follow to make sure it goes the right way. You don't want this to turn into the night where you guys fought over affirmative action and wound up not speaking to each other on the way home. It's your job to set the tone for the night and make sure there is as much date-like flirtation as possible. One way you can do this is by guiding the conversation where you want it to go. Think of yourself as the pilot of the plane. On this night, you want to fly your friend right into the sunset, where they will hold their breath and announce, "This is the most beautiful sky I have ever seen!" You want to steer them right into breathlessness.

Keep it light. This is the night you want to see your friend laughing every five seconds. Laughter is the best aphrodisiac. You know that feeling you get when you've been laughing so hard you can't catch your breath and your cheeks hurt? That's the same feeling you get after some crazy mind-blowing sex. It's that "glow." You want your friend to feel that after a night with you. But this is not the time to practice your amateur comedy act. Don't pull out a bunch of your grandfather's jokes. This is the night to show them how amazing your sense of humor is. Be flirty, and don't be afraid to make fun of yourself a little. Share with them the things that you find most amusing. Or relive a memory you both have shared that always makes you bust up when you think about it, like that time the substitute teacher's coffee got spiked with laxatives. Whatever you do, keep the conversation fun.

Avoid politics and serious topics. Now is not the time to share with your friend all the details about your cat's death or the gruesome murder trial your dad's working on. That's fine for when you are really dating each other; then, of course, you shouldn't hold anything back. As friends, you've shared everything—maybe too much, because you're where you are, right? So on this date, stay away from any downer or buzzkill topics. Also steer clear of controversial issues and politics: abortion, taxes, the recession . . . . Even if you're an unemployed, pro-choice activist who doesn't pay taxes, keep that to yourself and talk about butterflies. There are so many great topics for you two to discuss—another time. Not tonight. Save that stuff for your online message boards. Tonight is just about the two of you, so keep it that way.

Play games. We're not talking "hard to get," but rather the games that you would play with your friends during a long car ride. Would You Rather? is a good one. You can also do hypotheticals, like "If you could have one superpower, what would it be?" or "If you could have dinner with anyone in the whole world, who would you pick?" It may sound silly, but playing little games like this is a stealth way of flirting. It will show them you're fun and creative, and you'll learn new things about each other in the process.

Tell them one personal story that shows a lot about you. Another objective for you on this date is to build intimacy between you. It's a hard thing to pin down, but one way you can get it flowing is to share something personal with your friend, something that you haven't told them before. Now, don't get all dark and deep. Save that part about finding out your parents were drug dealers for another time. But share something cute—maybe your terrible first kiss or best family vacation, or your favorite childhood memory. This will make them feel like they are seeing a different side of you, and that you're letting them in.

Share a funny anecdote about them. One universal rule about people is that everybody likes to talk about themselves. Adding on to that, they like it even more when other people talk about them. So tell your friend something you've noticed about them. It can be an observation, like "I've noticed you always bite your lip when you're nervous," or it can be teasing, as in, "I've never met anyone who pays more attention to *US Weekly* than you do," or it can be sincere: "You have this way of making anyone around you feel special." But don't lay it on too thick. Don't shower them with compliments; just offer one or two little observations that will show your friend that you know them better than anyone else and that you really care about them. You can also share a funny story, like, "The first time I saw you, I thought you were so stuck-up." As long as you follow it with, "But now I know you're not."

Ask questions. They can be about anything—music, travel, dreams, memories, etc. You guys already know all the day-to-day things about each other because you've lived it together. So go into unknown territory. Ask your friend, "What was the best concert

you ever went to?" or "What was your first memory as a child?"
After they answer, tell them yours too so it doesn't seem like
you're interviewing them for *People* magazine. What you're looking for here is a connection that you didn't know was there before.
You want that moment of discovery where they say, "You've always
wanted to go on an African safari? Me too!" Just because you're
friends doesn't mean you already know everything there is to know
about each other. There's always more to uncover and, as you
leave Friend Zone territory and cross over into Relationship Land,
you are going to need to know these things.

Listen. This one should be a no-brainer, but you'd be surprised
how many people are terrible listeners. If you're going to do all
this work and come up with these brilliant questions, then you'd
better listen to the answers. Not only will it be useful down the
road when you have to come up with a one-year anniversary gift
for them, but it will help you keep the conversation flowing. If you

Conversation Topics

GOOD = Childhood games

BAD = Childhood trauma

GOOD = What their parents do

BAD = Where's their real dad?

GOOD = Best concert ever

BAD = Best sex ever

GOOD = Next place they want to travel

BAD = Famine of South Sudan

GOOD = Favorite pet

BAD = How it died

GOOD = Career goals

BAD = Cancer

really listen, then one piece of information they give you about their favorite vacation spot growing up will lead you to ask if they have been back to that tire swing since, and then before you know it, you are planning a road trip together. Just don't get so wrapped up in thinking about what you should say next that you forget to listen to them. Relax, take a deep breath, and trust that you know how to have a conversation.

HOW TO FLIRT

If you do one thing and one thing only on this night, *flirt*. Flirt like the kids are hungry and the rent is due. This is the key to taking this night and making it more than just two people hanging out (which was your main problem before). That means smile. All the time. Even if it hurts. Laugh. Even if what they said is not that funny. It was funny to you! Hilarious, in fact. Touch them—your hand on top of theirs, or hold their hand, or brush their arm with yours. (We'll get into more on touching in the next chapter.) Make eye contact, lean in close, compliment them. If you think you are bad at flirting, believe us, that's all in your head.

Flirting is crucial on this night, because you are sending a message: that you are doable. Not that you're going to sleep with your friend, because that's too much for a first date, but that you are a doable person, in the general sense.

The moon is above you, the fireflies are glowing, and everything is going perfectly. But you can't sit back and congratulate yourself quite yet, because there's one thing you still need to do on this night, and believe us, you *have* to do it.

⁘⁘⁘⁘⁘⁘⁘

Dear Wing Girls:

I am soooooo happy! I went on a date last night with this guy who I had been in the Friend Zone with forever. I had always dreamed about going on a date with him, but I never thought it would happen! I've been following all your advice and it totally worked! I made sure it didn't feel like we were just hanging out, because we used to do that all the time. I had my friend do my makeup and I made sure to dress cute, and when he picked me up, he was blown away! We had the best time! We held hands during the concert and he was really flirty. It was the best date ever!!!

⁘⁘⁘⁘⁘⁘⁘

CHAPTER 10
Making the Move

The biggest thing you need to do on the Date is make a move. If you don't, you could become trapped in the Friend Zone all over again. After all, the Move is what separates friends from lovers. Most of the time, the moment leading up to the Move makes you feel like you're a pirate walking the plank or a soldier going into battle. There are a series of steps that you can take to prepare for it, and we're going to walk you through each of them. In case you haven't already figured it out, the Move is physical contact during your date: handholding, touching, and kissing. In other words, the good stuff.

Liam made the Date with Nora really look and feel like one: restaurant, candles, a moonlight walk, the whole deal. Unfortunately, he still felt that grabbing a girl and kissing her, especially Nora, was a violation. He felt like it would be overstepping her boundaries—even though she was batting her eyelashes, gazing into his eyes, and flirting with him. At one point in the evening, she even said she really liked him. For some reason, Liam couldn't get his body out of the Friend Zone long enough to pull Nora in and give her a smooch. He used a lot of reasoning to talk himself out of making the Move. He told himself the first date would not be a good time to kiss her and that he could do it another time. Unfortunately, he had been telling himself similar lies for the past five years of their "friendship," and he was really starting to piss Nora off. She didn't get it. Was he missing a tongue? Did he have lip fungus? What did she have to do to get a kiss around here? Liam really blew it. By not breaking out of his comfort zone for even a minute, he turned Nora off him for good.

AFFECTION DURING THE DATE

Have you ever played that game with your friends (or yourself) where you stare at two strangers in a restaurant and try to tell if they're friends or lovers? The minute one of them reaches over and strokes the other's arm, the game is over. Because they touched. Isn't that the one thing that separates friends from lovers? It's all the touching lovers do. So there's your answer, the secret you've been looking for this whole time. If you don't touch your friend on your date, you are going to wind up exactly where you've been—do we even need to say it? In the Friend Zone.

In order to send the message loud and clear that this is a date, you need to show some affection. You need to touch your friend. It needs to be more than a punch on the arm or a pat on the back. We're talking handholding, arm grazing, cheek brushing, and hair stroking.

You should know that it's going to feel awkward and unnatural. It's weird to sit across from someone you've known for a long time and think, "How do I touch them in a way that seems really spontaneous and normal but that also sends the message that I care about them as more than a friend?" Do it wrong and it can be as awkward as bringing your parents on a date. But if you do it right, it's the best way to signal to them that you like them in a sexy way, and that you'd like to touch more than just their knee. It's also a good way to spark a little something in your friend, a little curiosity about touching more of you, or a reminder that you are a sexual person. These are good things. You want them to feel this way.

The thing you need to remember is that even if it feels really awkward to you, as long as you own it and play it off like you're not weirded out by it, your friend won't be either. They will take their cues from you. So if you're sitting side by side, put your arm around your friend, or if you're a girl, pull his arm around your shoulders. If you're at dinner across from each other, put your hand on theirs. If the moment is right, do the eyelash move—you know, the one where you go, "Oh, hold on, you have an eyelash right there." And then you take it and put it on your finger and tell them to make a wish. Other good signs of affection are playing with their hair, holding their hand, touching their face, rubbing their back, etc. Some to avoid: poking, pinching, hitting, biting—basically anything your little brother would do.

Another thing we need to say about affection: a little goes a long way. You don't have to spend the whole night caressing their neck. Use it sparingly, as a way of increasing the sexual tension between you. After all, this is your first date. So don't give away the grand prize before the drawing.

PRESSURE TEST

One way to figure out where your date stands on the whole issue of touching you is something we call the Pressure Test. It's really simple. You press a body part of yours against theirs. If the other person likes you and wants you to touch them, they will push back. If they aren't into it, they will pull away.

A good time to try this test is when you're sitting side by side, like at a movie theater, or in the backseat of a cab. You can press your knee against theirs and see if they press back or not. Or if your friend's hand is on an armrest, you can press your hand against theirs. Make sure you are pressing lightly. If an outsider were looking at the two of you, they wouldn't see any movement. That's how subtle it is.

The Pressure Test

STEP ONE: Lay your hand close to your friend's hand, on an armrest if you are sitting. If you are standing or walking side by side, then let your hand dangle close to theirs.

STEP TWO: Gently push the side of your hand against theirs. Make it seem like an accident. Keep your hand there, putting a tiny bit of pressure against their hand.

STEP THREE: Wait a second to see if they move their hand or if they pull away.

STEP FOUR: If they don't move their hand, then slide your hand under theirs, facing up. If you're walking, put your palm against theirs.

STEP FIVE: Curl your fingers and hold their hand!

Once you've tried this out, any time they push back or even if they stay where they are and don't pull away, that is a green light to keep going. By the end of the night, you will be making the Move!

HOLDING HANDS

Mary didn't think of Charlie as anything more than a friend. They weren't ever best friends, but they were close growing up because they did theater together. One day, Charlie asked her to go to the city with his family and friends. Mary didn't think twice about it, because they had always just been friends. They had a nice dinner and then everyone split up, and all the younger people went out to a bar. The bar had patio seating and Charlie told her to sit by him, which, again, she really didn't think about. Then the strangest thing happened. Charlie held her hand! It totally caught her off guard. She'd known him since they were twelve and never really thought of him in that way. It turned her world upside down.

The thing is, when you hold someone's hand, you are telling them that you feel a certain way about them, that you like them in a way that friends don't like each other. It's the world's simplest way of saying "I like you." Mary might not have ever considered Charlie had he not worked up the courage to grab her hand. It made her think about what it would be like to kiss him or be with him. Even though he didn't explicitly say how he felt about her, she saw him in a completely new way after that, as someone who could be more than a friend, maybe even a boyfriend.

Any talk of handholding may give you fifth-grade flashbacks of papier-mâché art projects and kickball at recess. But the thing is, adults hold hands too. That's still step one in making a physical connection with someone. As a grown-up, you'll take it farther than "Let's sit next to each other at lunch and you can drink my chocolate milk," but you're still going to start with holding your friend's hand, so don't go thinking you're too advanced for this.

Believe it or not, there's a technique to handholding. Yes, it's simple, but there's still a right way to do it.

For guys: When you are with her, wait until you are seated near her, either at a table, on a couch, or in a movie theater. Then, lay your hand next to hers (palm down) and inch it over, placing your hand on top of hers. If she doesn't pull away, link your fingers with hers. Then turn it over so that her hand is on top. If she lets you do this, then you're on the right track.

For girls: Get him to grab your hand. You can do this by initiating contact, with something from this bag of tricks:

1. See whose hands are bigger—say that you have really small hands or notice that he has really big hands, then measure yours against his.

2. Challenge him to a game of thumb war.

3. Read his palm, or if you don't know how, make it up.

4. Ask if he's ever had a manicure. Then examine his nails.

5. Lay your arm next to him or brush it against his.

If you try these and he doesn't grab the opportunity, then at that point, you've got to take matters into your own hands, literally. Grab his hand. Put your hand on top of his and link fingers. If he lets you do this and doesn't pull away, then he's into you, because guys usually won't hold hands with girls unless they like them.

READ THEIR BODY LANGUAGE

Body language is cryptic. If you knew how to read it, you wouldn't have spent all these days, months, and years in sexual purgatory with your friend. There are a few no-brainers when it comes to body language.

READING GIRLS' BODY LANGUAGE

There are some easy ways to tell if she's into you on this date:

She's making eye contact. This one's pretty easy to figure out. If she's spending all her time staring at the other people in the restaurant and only glances your way every hour or so, then her attention is not on you. However, if her eyeballs are following you like that creepy painting in the haunted mansion, then you're in luck. The more eye contact, the better.

She's leaning in. If she's leaning toward you, then guess what she's not doing? Trying to get as far away from you as humanly possible. When a girl is into a guy, she wants to be close to him—she can't help it—so pay attention to the distance between you two.

She plays with her hair. If she's playing with her hair, or tossing it like a girl in a Pantene commercial, then you are a certified stud. Any kind of hair play is a girl's way of primping for a guy. Most of the time she doesn't even know she is doing it. So watch for her signature hair flip to know what's going on inside her head.

Her body is facing you. If she likes you, then she'll open up her body toward you. Pay attention to the way she's sitting. Are her knees pointing toward you under the table? If you look, don't make it obvious. If she's crossing her arms over her chest, then she's worried you will try to touch her.

Also, be aware what your body language is telling her. A lot of these things are the same for girls and guys. So make sure you're giving her your full attention, that your body faces her, and that you lean in toward her. Or you can just wear a sign that says "Let's Get It On," and then we can all go home early.

READING GUYS' BODY LANGUAGE

Guys are easy to read if you know what to look for. Here are some telltale signs that he's interested in you:

He's making eye contact. Guys have short attention spans, so don't expect him to be gazing into your orbs for hours and hours. That would be scary anyway. The question is: Where does he focus most of his attention? If his eyes spend most of the time following the girl across the restaurant whose sweater is two sizes too small, and only dart over to you when you sneeze, then he's distracted. But if a guy is into you, his attention will keep coming back to you, no matter how many tight sweaters walk by.

His body faces yours. When a guy likes you, he inadvertently turns his whole body your way. One way to check is to see which way his feet are pointing. If his toes always point directly at you, then he's smitten.

He gets in close. When you see people in love, as much of their bodies as possible are touching. Their heads are together, they're holding hands, and they're pressed against each other. It's like they're trying to become one person. So when a guy likes you, he tries to get as close to you as he can. He's going to lean in, he's going to slide his chair next to yours, and he's going to get his face up in your face. On the other hand, if he doesn't like you, his body is going to show it by being as far away from you as possible.

He smiles a lot. Guys show sexual attraction by flashing their pearly whites. Maybe it goes back to the caveman days where they had to bare their teeth to fight off saber-toothed tigers. If your guy smiles all the time when he's near you—genuinely smiles—then he's having a good time.

He has a boner. Sorry, but we had to go there. If you give a guy a stiffy just by sitting next to him, then you are good at your job. Congrats.

There are some things you can do for him so that he can read what your body is saying. You need to tell him as obviously as you can, without actually saying it, that you want him to kiss you. He is going to look to you for the signals that say it's okay for him to make a move. Remember to open your body toward him. If you're hunched over and hugging yourself like you're in a straitjacket, that doesn't send the message for him to come over there and ravish you. You need to sit up straight and keep your arms at your sides. If you're sitting, point your knees toward him and tilt your head in his direction. Also, what your eyes say is important. If you think to yourself, "Kiss me, come on, kiss me," it will show in your eyes. But if you think, "Come on, you coward, what are you waiting for? Hurry up and kiss me before my eightieth birthday," that will show in your eyes as well, and he might get scared and run away.

KISSING

Everyone's had a bad kiss, it happens, but tonight we don't need anything getting in the way of your chemistry. If the kiss is bad, it's going to confirm for your friend that the Friend Zone is where you belong. What you need to aim for is a kiss that is sexy and fun. You want the kiss to make your friend think bad things about you, in a good way. Here's how:

For guys, it's your job to kiss her. You are the one who's going to lean in and give the girl a kiss. You don't want her to question her feelings for you again, do you? So be the aggressor, as hard as that is for you. And for girls, you must do everything in your power to get that kiss. If it doesn't happen from him, you'll have to bite the bullet and do it yourself. The thing to remember, no matter who you are, is that you aren't leaving this date without swappin' some spit. If you can't bring yourself to do it, then you can't have a boyfriend or a girlfriend. That's the choice: either kiss or turn back into a frog friend.

Right before the kiss or after you eat something, take a quick trip to the bathroom. No matter what you ate or didn't eat, nerves can give you bad breath, so chomp on a mint or use a breath strip. No matter how much someone likes you, if your breath smells like rotted beet juice, they won't want a kiss. Also put on some color-less lip balm to make sure your lips are soft and kissable. But remember, don't do any of this in front of your friend.

"But when will I do this?!" You will kiss your friend when you are at the end of the date. You will do it in the car before dropping them off, or at their door, old-fashioned '80s-teen-movie style. Make sure that wherever it is, the lighting is right and there is an escape route. Even if the kiss is the best thing on earth, you want to be able to drive off or go into your house immediately following it. You want your kiss to be the last thing on their mind.

Right before the kiss, you may want to compliment your friend, but again, don't get overly romantic about it. If they make a joke, then you can say they are funny. If your friend looks really good, then you can say that too. But if you want to give them an over-the-top compliment, like "I love what a wonderful person you are," keep it to yourself. By staying in the present moment, you will keep your friend from thinking about the old you. Instead, they'll just focus on what a great time they're having and how they don't want the night to end.

THE LAST RESORT (FOR GIRLS)

If you've been sitting in his car for half an hour and he keeps droning on and on about the Mets, then you might have to step it up and do his job for him. He might feel like kissing you is taboo, that your lips are forbidden. So he may not try anything with you. If this happens, no biggie. You can kiss him. He will probably be very grateful that you did. But once you kiss him, stop. Your job is done. Let him take it from there and turn it into a make out session or kiss you again. Because of your previous experience in the Friend Zone, you can't make a habit out of making the move for him. One kiss to break the ice is okay, but more than that and you have to ask yourself, "Does he even like me?" And aren't you sick of asking yourself that question already?

THE KISS: WHAT NOT TO DO

Now you know that you are not leaving this date without a kiss on the lips. To up your chances of having the best kiss possible, here are some classic kissing mistakes to avoid:

Don't ask permission! Asking permission is about the lamest thing you can do before you go in for a move. You don't want your friend to think twice about it. You want it to just happen, and asking permission ruins all the fun.

Don't let them know you're uncomfortable! Even if you would rather swallow razor blades than make the move, don't show it. Showing how uncomfortable you are really ruins the moment.

Your friend needs to know they are in good hands. So even though you feel all squirmy-wormy inside and want to die, don't let them see you sweat.

Don't keep talking until you work up the courage! The worst thing you can do in this situation is to become a Talky McTalkerson. Believe us, the more you talk, the less attracted to you your friend is becoming. So keep it brief, try not to say too much, and let your body do the talking.

Don't drag it out! Get in and get out. Don't make it a big, long, shaky nightmare. The faster it is, the better, because after the initial kiss, you are good to go and you won't feel half as nervous as you did before. In fact, if you do it right, you'll feel like a million bucks, or, at least, you'll feel major relief.

Don't apologize for how bad you are at this! Self-deprecation has a time and a place, and this is not it. Again, your friend needs to feel they are in good hands. If you are saying what an awkward nerd you are, that doesn't leave much room for chemistry. You are a totally confident human being, or at least you are pretending to be.

Don't make jokes! If talking is bad, then making jokes is much worse. You've made enough jokes. That's what landed you in the "I don't take this person seriously" category in the first place, so don't go back there. Instead, move on to the "this person is dead sexy" category, where you belong.

Don't mention their ex or yours! This one is so obvious, it pains us to write it down, but pretty please with a cherry on top, don't mention anyone either of you has been with before. It's best not

Top Five Worst Kisses

1. AMBUSH KISS: When you attack your friend's face without fair warning. Your lips are everywhere—not just on theirs, but all over their face. They have no idea what you are going to do next, and so they just wait it out in horror.

2. OXYGEN MASK: When you kiss your friend by putting your mouth over the top of their nose, like an oxygen mask.

3. DENTAL HYGIENIST: When you lick and kiss your friend's teeth instead of their lips.

4. OPEN CAVITY KISS: When you kiss without closing your mouth. You make an O-shape with your mouth and never use your tongue.

5. ATTACK OF THE LIPS: When your friend is talking and you kiss them mid-sentence.

to talk about anyone but the two of you during this point in the Date anyway.

Don't get too romantic! This is not the time to bust out the feather and caress their face with it. Basic real-life moves work best. You are not in a Shakespeare play, so knock it off with the poems and the sonnets. Just lean in and do your business.

Don't force yourself on them if they're not into it! If you've already gone in for the Move and they are cringing and pulling away, it's best to stop throwing yourself at them. If you feel like it didn't go well and they are pulling away in disgust, keep acting like the sexy thing that you are but back up and don't push any more action.

WHY NOTHING MORE THAN KISSING?

Melissa and Tony did something really bad. They slept together on their first date. Melissa thought Tony didn't like her, so she stayed in the Friend Zone for years. Then one day, she realized that waiting in the wings with no hobbies or passions would be unattractive to anyone, so she started making independent films and submitting them to festivals and hasn't looked back since. She realized she needed something she loved even more than Tony, and she found it. She did everything right, and Tony, who had always thought Melissa was pretty, finally became attracted to her. On their first date, they were so overcome by passion that they ended up having sex. They were legal adults, almost twenty-eight, and had slept with their fair share of people, sometimes on the first date, so what was the big deal? The big deal was that they already knew everything about each other intellectually, and now

Top Five Things Not to Say Before a Kiss

- "I SHOULDN'T HAVE EATEN ALL THOSE ONION RINGS."
- "HERE GOES NOTHING."
- "YOU GO TO THE LEFT, I'LL GO TO THE RIGHT."
- "WANNA SWAP SPIT?"
- "I APOLOGIZE IN ADVANCE FOR WHAT I'M ABOUT TO DO."

they knew everything physically as well. Now it was weird, because after one date they were in a full-fledged relationship with no room to grow.

For friends, things have to be taken much more slowly than in other relationships because you know each other better than any two strangers who met online. Once you go there physically, there's not much left to learn about each other. Since you've been in the Friend Zone with this person, you already have a deep emotional connection. Once you add the physical element, you skip all the steps that would naturally build a relationship. It's like going from zero to sixty. If you do anything other than kiss on that first night, you really screw yourself. Even if you've slept with everyone on the planet and so has your friend, stick with kissing so that you'll have room to grow.

IF THEY DON'T KISS YOU BACK

If you go in for the kiss and your friend doesn't reciprocate, that's on them. You did everything right, you followed the plan, so don't walk away from this blaming yourself. You're not going to win every game you play. But at least you stepped up to bat. The only thing you can take away from this is that tonight wasn't the night. It doesn't mean it's never going to happen. It doesn't mean you gross them out. It just means your friend hasn't come around quite yet. Don't give up hope, but now you have to go back to Chapter 5: The Separation and see what else you can do. Some people just take longer to change their minds and to stop seeing you as "just a friend" and start seeing you as a sexy lover. If it's worth giving it another try—and it probably is, because you've done so much work so far—give it another go. Chalk this one up to an off night and ask your friend out again later on, and go in for the kiss on that date. If it still doesn't work, then it is time for you to move on. But make sure that you give it the old college try.

If you've gotten this far, then we need to take a moment to pat you on the back. This is truly the hardest part of the Date. Everyone—whether they're in the Friend Zone or not—absolutely dreads having to make the Move. Some people spend their whole adult lives psyching themselves out about it, and the longer they wait, the harder it becomes to do it. The whole outcome of the date rests on that one question: Did they or did they not make the Move? If they didn't, then no matter how great the rest of the date was, no matter how much you laughed or how much you had in common, when your friends ask how it went, you're just going to say, "Okay." Because without some lip-locking at the end of the date, how can it be more than okay? It's like a gigantic question that never got answered. "We totally hit it off . . . We had such a good time, we were flirting, it was so fun. BUT—do we have any chemistry?" That's a huge question that has just been tabled for another time. Anyone who goes on a date without making a move puts themselves at risk of falling into the Friend Zone. That's why for you, not making a move was not even an option. You had to do it. And you did.

You overcame a major hurdle, and this is a huge turning point in your relationship with your friend. No matter what happens from here on out, we guarantee they will think of you differently, a good kind of different. You're no longer wishy-washy. You're no longer paralyzed by fear. You're no longer the person who asks permission for everything. Now you're a doer. You go out and get what you want. You grab the bull by the horns. That's the kind of person you are. Now you've done the one essential action that separates people in the Friend Zone from everyone in the rest of the world. You made a move! Yay for you! You did it! But you're not completely out of the danger zone yet. One good night can't erase years and years of habits and behavior that got you into the Friend Zone in the first place. You can't throw everything you've learned out the window quite yet. You still have some work to do. But now you can see the finish line. You're almost there!

CHAPTER 11

What's Next?

So you've had your date and your mind-blowing kiss; now what? Well, first things first: *hide this book*. The worst thing that could happen in the early stages of dating is your friend finding a book on how you got them to date you. As helpful as this book is, your friend may not find it so amusing.

This is the stage where a lot of you might get a little panicky. "Okay, I can fake it for one date, but how do I keep from confessing my love to this person now that we are seeing each other more regularly?" Or maybe even, "How do I avoid acting like their friend again and not turn every day into a hang-out?" Well, don't worry your pretty little never-going-back-to-the-Friend-Zone head about that. We will show you how to take what you've learned and apply it to dating and even a relationship with your friend. It may feel so easy to creep back into your old lying-around-the-house routine with your friend, but you two need to start from absolute scratch and erase everything you've done prior to this. Pretend you just met online yesterday. Would you go to the house of someone you just met? No! Would you feel comfortable not planning dates and just winging it around someone you hardly know? No, you wouldn't!

DATING YOUR FRIEND

You need to make sure each date is as date-like and exciting as the first one. You can't throw in the towel yet; remember, you are still proving to them that you are a sexual being, not a buddy they can take for granted. This takes planning and some thought. Make sure you're still doing fun things. The whole problem with your relationship before was that you were too comfortable with each other, so you have to start over. You need to dress up for each other, get nervous before you hang out, and say good-bye at their door with a kiss.

KEEPING THE MOMENTUM OF THE FIRST DATE

Stay away from each other's houses. Home is not where the heart is until you are in an official relationship. The home can be a lazy place to be. Your objective here is to build the passion, and if you're sitting on the couch together eating chocolate-covered raisins, that's the last thing you're going to be doing. Nothing says "I give up" like the two of you staring into a screen together. Try to keep computers, TV, and phones out of your relationship time right now. Movie theaters are okay as long as you don't go every day of the week. Try to do something active where you can really connect through actually doing something, not staring at other people doing something.

THE POWER BALANCE

Layla and Ryan used to be in the Friend Zone. Ryan was in deep. He did everything for Layla. If she wanted Chinese food in the middle of the night, he'd bring her moo shu pork. After a lot of hard work, he got out of the Friend Zone and they started dating. He thought all his problems would disappear. He hoped that now

Is It Equal?

IT'S UNEQUAL...

- IF YOU ONLY HANG OUT WITH THEIR FRIENDS.
- IF YOUR FRIEND MAKES YOU TAG ALONG TO THEIR ACTIVITIES BUT DOESN'T COME TO YOURS.
- IF YOUR FRIEND WANTS YOU TO GIVE ADVICE ALL THE TIME.
- IF YOUR FRIEND NEVER ASKS YOU HOW YOUR DAY WAS.
- IF YOU FIND YOURSELF CONSTANTLY RUNNING ERRANDS FOR YOUR FRIEND.

they would have a more equal relationship. Maybe Layla would get him the moo shu every once in a while. Unfortunately, Ryan was still working with his same old bag of tricks. He still worshipped Layla, and she still relied on him for everything and didn't give him anything in return. They ended up breaking up, because they had both expected things to go differently once they were in a real relationship. Layla had hoped that Ryan would stop placing her on a pedestal and put his foot down once in a while. And Ryan had hoped that Layla would go out of her way for him. Whatever promise they both saw during the Separation and the Date quickly went out the window once they got into a relationship.

The relationship is the crucial point where you either fall back into your old roles with each other or assume new roles. Sure, you could fall back on the way things used to be: your friend taking main stage while you provide the witty repartee and fetch their coffee. That's how you used to roll, back when your friend would rather swim through a sea of sewage than let you tongue-kiss them. Do you really want to act out that scenario again? No! You want them to want you with the force of a thousand gods, or at least a couple hundred. So keep it equal. If you feel yourself slipping, get back on the horse, pick up your sword, and take a good look at what's unbalanced and correct it.

WHEN DO WE GET TO HAVE SEX?

You've already waited so long; why not wait until you are connected as boyfriend and girlfriend before you seal the deal? You need to get to the point where your friend is shouting your relationship status from the rooftops or else you have a real possibility of flying right back into the Friend Zone. Sex should be the frosting on the relationship cake, not the filling. So even though you wanted to take their clothes off from the moment you laid your little eyes on them, take it down a notch and really get to know them first. Just like we said not to have sex on the first date, now we're saying to hold off until your relationship is official. That means a monogamous relationship where you introduce each other as girlfriend and boyfriend and use the L-word. You don't want to skip the dating part and go right to being an old married couple by having sex too early. Pace yourself!

KEEP YOUR COOL

"Great! Now that we're together I can pull out all these poems I've written about my friend! I can finally let loose and tell them what a freaky stalker I've been!" Do not, as hard as it may be, get all lovey-dovey until you've established that your friend is in love with you too. Most people feel that they need to earn that kind of admiration as the other person really gets to know them, and even though you felt you knew your friend before, you didn't. Knowing someone as a friend is far different from knowing someone as a boyfriend or girlfriend. You knew the version of your friend that you wanted them to be. Now, without projecting all of those expectations on your friend, you can finally know them for who they really are, so you can love them in a more mature, less fantasy-based way.

SLOW YOUR ROLL

You may be champing at the bit to get this thing solid and squared away, but you must take it slow. You already know this person so well, it feels strange to actually go on dates and say good night at the front door, but that's the way it has to go for you. This is not a normal situation, and when it comes to your friend, you are not normal. You wanted to get married the second you laid eyes on this person, so why on earth would you stop the train now that you are this close? Because your overenthusiasm was a turnoff in the first place. So again, play it cool, and take your time.

LET THEM MEET YOU HALFWAY

When it comes to planning your dates and making an effort toward romance, you can't be the one doing all the work. That's what you used to do, but now you have someone to share that job with. You are done with your solo orchestration of the Love Show. Yes, you still need to put effort in, but so does your friend. Sure, you wanted to get the puppy, but you have to remember that they did too. When your friend starts getting lazy, you can't jump in and do everything. You have to let them set up dates and plan things. You made it easy for them to be lazy in the past, and how did that work out for you? Let them put some effort in this time.

Warning Signs That You're Slipping Back into the Friend Zone

- YOUR FRIEND DOESN'T CONSIDER YOU WHEN THEY MAKE PLANS.
- YOUR FRIEND TALKS ABOUT OTHER PEOPLE THEY'RE INTO.
- YOUR FRIEND EXPECTS YOU TO DO THINGS FOR THEM ALL THE TIME (PICK THEM UP, BUY THEM THINGS, HELP THEM MEET DEADLINES).
- YOUR FRIEND DOESN'T RESPOND TO TEXTS AND PHONE CALLS, AND THEY DON'T CALL YOU BACK.

MAKING IT A REAL RELATIONSHIP

A caterpillar eventually turns into a butterfly, a tadpole turns into a frog, Pinocchio turns into a real boy, and now you get to take your baby relationship and turn it into a real, living, breathing, official relationship. This is what you spent night after sleepless night fantasizing about way back in the day when you were stuck in Friend Zone hell. But you should know that a real relationship is not a fantasy. There are good times and bad times, and it's a lot of hard work. It's not all roses and rainbows. Guess we should have told you that before you went to all this trouble, huh? But the good news is, this person started out as your friend. You knew them on their good days and on their get-the-hell-away-from-me-I'm-in-a-fight-with-my-coworker-and-taking-it-out-on-you days. You guys have already been through a lot together, so if you made it this far, then you know what you're signing up for. Everybody wants their lover to be their best friend, and you're lucky because you started out as best friends and made it to lovers. So you're looking at the real deal here.

MAKING IT OFFICIAL

You should be dating for at least three months before you make your relationship official. That way you can be sure you've given it a good test drive. Here's how you know it's time to go there: your friend is as invested in the relationship as you are. They make plans with you, they talk about the future using the word "us," not just "me," and they hint that they don't want to date anyone else. If you can check all these things off the list, then you two need to have the "what are we" talk. You have to be clear and spell it out. You need to figure out the terms.

This is when you say you don't want them to date anyone else and that you don't want to date anyone else either. You want to introduce them as your boyfriend or girlfriend. Make sure that's what

Dating Timeline

- ONE DATE A WEEK FOR A MONTH IN A PUBLIC AREA, CUDDLING.
- AFTER A MONTH, SEE EACH OTHER TWICE A WEEK.
- AFTER THREE MONTHS, MAKE IT OFFICIAL.

they want too. Then you change your Facebook status from "it's complicated" to "in a relationship" and then all your friends and family click the Like button, and then your parents turn to each other and say, "Did you ever think that would happen? No? Neither did I!" and they think to themselves what a great job they did raising you and what a catch you turned out to be.

YOU DON'T HAVE TO HIDE YOUR FEELINGS ANYMORE

Once it's official, you don't have to hold back as much as you did before. You can tell them how you really feel. At this point, you shouldn't have to worry about scaring your friend off. You can be all lovey-dovey and call each other pet names like "Mooshie" and make your other friends roll their eyes. But remember to always make sure your actions are being reciprocated. If you're skywriting their name from a plane but they still haven't told their best friend that you two are dating, there's a problem.

POWER NEEDS TO BE BALANCED

The power balance is important here. In a long-term, serious relationship, it needs to go back and forth. The amount of work you each put in to make the other person happy should be equal. The amount of affection shown between you two should be about the same. If your friends can look at your relationship and say, "Wow, you're wrapped around their finger," then you don't have enough power and you need to get some. If there is an imbalance of power in the long run, you are in danger of slipping back into the Friend Zone, and you have come too far and worked too hard to let that happen. So don't.

IF IT'S JUST NOT WORKING

If, even after you've made it official and exchanged the L-word, you find that your friend is still backing away, talking to you about other people they think are cute, not looking in your general direction, and squinting in pain every time you pay them a compliment, then at this point we say: their problem, not yours. Some people are messed up and are scared of someone who is actually available. Maybe love and affection freak them out. Maybe they didn't have enough love in their childhood and they feel they don't deserve someone who is nice to them and wants more than anything to make them happy. Maybe they are so self-loathing that they think that anyone who shows love for them must be a total idiot. People like this do exist in this world, and if you are unfortunate enough to have spent your life trying to make one of them love you, at a certain point you have to get off the bus before they steer that bus to the point of no return with both of you on it. If this is the case, you need to know it's not anything you did wrong. This is their issue, and they need professional counseling to figure out what is up with them. You don't need to sit there and wait for that. You've waited long enough, and it's time to cut the cord.

GOOD FOR YOU

Maybe you are 100 percent out of the Friend Zone now, maybe you have a toe out and the rest of your feet are still in, or maybe it hasn't worked for you yet. Wherever you are now, you are a million times better off than where you were when you started reading this book—a million. Why? Because now you have clarity. You are not wandering around in the pitch-black wilderness without a flashlight. You shined a light on your situation and saw it for what it was—the good, the bad, and the ugly—and now you have, at the very least, the truth. You risked it all, did the work, and saw it through. Think back to the very beginning, when you picked up this book for the first time. Remember how pathetic you felt? We are so glad you got out of that hole. Seriously, look how far you've come. You stood up for yourself and actually took action to make a change. Maybe you thought you were doing it for your friend, but in the end, you did it for yourself—and that is something to be proud of. Now you know you deserve better than sitting in the backseat while your friend makes out with someone else in the front. And guess what? You're never, ever, ever going to let that happen again. In the next chapter we'll make sure of that.

Hey Wing Girls!
Okay, so I have been dating my former Friend Zone guy for the last couple months. It's like a dream come true! But I did what you said because I knew that if I acted all lovey-dovey and got too clingy, he would get bored really fast. I made a rule for myself—I didn't tell him—that we could only go out twice a week. The other nights were for my friends or me-time. He basically wanted to move in together after a week, but I said no, that we had to take it slow. With sex too. I made him wait for three months, until he said "I love you." Things are going so good and I feel like our relationship is totally equal.

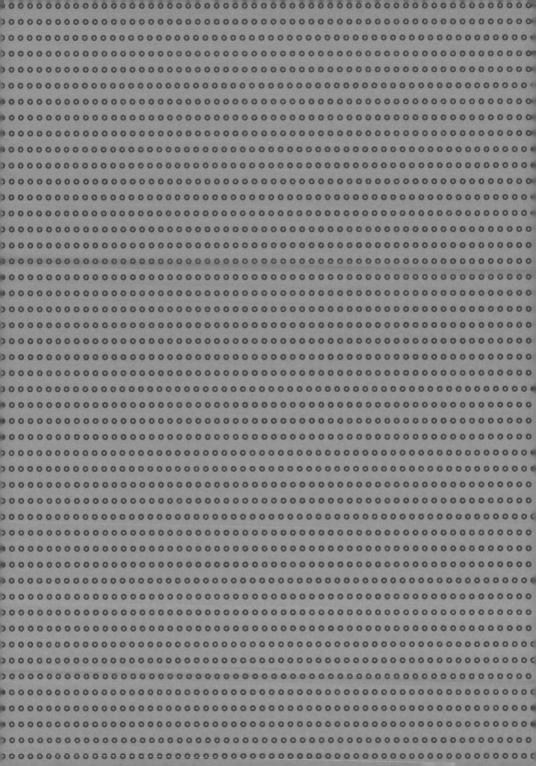

Part Four

. . . .

STAYING OUT OF THE FRIEND ZONE FOREVER

CHAPTER 12

How to Avoid the Friend Zone Forever

Getting out of the Friend Zone once is an incredible accomplishment, and if you did it, then you need to pat yourself on your own sexy back, because you're awesome. But before you break out the fireworks, you should know that staying out forever is going to take work on your part.

You have to fight the urge to go back into the Friend Zone every day of your ever-loving life. It's like learning to live with a chronic illness. You have to live with something we call Friendzone-itis. This means you're special. You can't do things the way normal people can. You have to live by a certain set of rules to help you break out of years of bad patterns. You can learn to live Friend Zone–free, but you have to remember: it's not a choice, it's a lifestyle. Following are The Friend Zone–Free Ten Commandments. Copy these down, tape them on your wall, memorize them, live them, love them, and eat them for breakfast.

1. THOU SHALT NOT BE FRIENDS WITH THE OPPOSITE SEX. Being friends with the opposite sex may work for other people, but not for you. Remember, you are special. As you now know, your Friend Zone brain is always tricking you and making you think that being someone's friend is the way to their heart. You need to

1. THOU SHALT NOT BE FRIENDS WITH THE OPPOSITE SEX.

2. THOU SHALT NOT GIVE IT AWAY FOR FREE.

3. THOU SHALT BACK THE TRUCK UP.

4. THOU SHALT NOT GIVE ADVICE.

5. THOU SHALT HAVE CLARITY.

6. THOU SHALT DO THY THANG.

7. THOU SHALT WORK THE SEXY.

8. THOU SHALT NOT BITCH, MOAN, AND COMPLAIN.

9. THOU SHALT NOT PUT ALL THY EGGS IN ONE BASKET.

10. THOU SHALT NOT SETTLE FOR LESS.

watch out for yourself and not befriend people that you'd rather be dating.

We don't want you to have to read this whole book all over again in three years when your friend from your running club has suddenly become your friend who had to move into your apartment when they got into a fight with the real love of their life—who is not you. Let's not go there. The easiest way to not go there? Don't be friends with people you secretly want to have an intimate roll in the hay with. It's one thing to have coffee with someone you are attracted to and are getting to know, but another to call that person a "good friend" when you already have trouble in that department to begin with.

Moral of the story? Stay away from the opposite sex. Those people are for dating, not for hanging out with and talking about your life's hopes and dreams.

2. THOU SHALT NOT GIVE IT AWAY FOR FREE.

Remember what a slave you were to your friend? Remember how you spent your life doing whatever they needed you to do? You were like their life-size wind-up doll, helping them move all weekend, driving them where they needed to go, housebreaking their Rottweiler while they were out partying the night away with their friends. Were you getting paid for any of that work, either in cold hard cash or sexual favors? No! You were giving away everything you had for nothing in return.

From now on, you will cross your heart and swear that you will never do that again—no trips to the airport, no favors, no giving advice late into the night—in fact, no giving advice whatsoever (see Commandment 4). Remember that your time is valuable— too valuable to be spending it hanging around someone, waiting for them to reward you with all the love and attention you deserve, when we all know that's never going to happen. Your time, your generosity—all of that is reserved for your life partner, not just anyone off the street (that is, your friend). If you ever find yourself in a position where everything you give is one-sided and you aren't getting anything in return, make like the building is on fire and *get yourself out of there.* We know you have a whole lot to give— you're a very generous, wonderful person—but no more giving without receiving.

3. THOU SHALT BACK THE TRUCK UP.

There is nothing less attractive than someone who's all up in your grill 24/7, and nothing will get you into the Friend Zone faster. So you need to back up, even when your Friend Zone brain screams, "I NEED TO BE ALL UP IN THEIR BUSINESS!" No, you don't. You don't need to invite yourself over, say you're available all day and night, and walk a foot behind them on the way to their desk.

Pretend every person of the opposite sex has a restraining order against you. If they initiate contact or conversation, then that's fine, but you don't need to call them every Thursday at 8 P.M. in the hopes of being invited to an all-night '80s movie marathon.

Now, if you are dating someone, this still applies until you are in a very committed, marriage-type situation. You can date all you want, but keep your human leech tendencies under control. Give them room to breathe and time to miss you.

4. THOU SHALT NOT GIVE ADVICE.

Think about all the time and energy you spent talking your friend through their life crisis of the moment: how you stayed up all night helping them figure out if they should join the Peace Corps or apply for that PhD program, how you made a list of pros and cons for them and put it into a PowerPoint presentation. How did that go for you? Did that get you into their pants? No, because no one wants to date their older sibling or therapist.

From now on, you are swallowing your well-meaning advice and keeping it to yourself. Your friend will have to find a new Dr. Phil, because you are not taking on any more clients. No more shoulder to cry on, no more late-night pep talks, no more "my dad never paid enough attention to me" secret-sharing. If you care about someone, you are going to have to stand by and watch as they make their own mistakes and figure things out for themselves. You are not on this earth to save them, protect them, or keep them from falling. They have family members to do that job. From now on, you save your hard-earned wisdom for the person who truly loves you back.

5. THOU SHALT HAVE CLARITY.

You will be clear in every interaction you have with the opposite sex. If you meet someone and you want to date them, you will say so. You will make it clear as the light of day that you are not in the business of making new friends. You hate friends; you like bona fide lovers. There shouldn't be any more late nights wondering what exactly is going on between you two, because it will all be out on the table. No, you don't need to spill your guts—in fact, don't— but you do need to make sure the other person knows you are interested in getting to know them in a dating way, not in a hang-out-ambiguously-all-night-hoping-you-end-up-spooning way.

Eventually, you need the other person to refer to you as someone they are dating, or, when the time comes, their boyfriend or girlfriend, not their friend. Being someone's vague "friend thingy" will not work for you anymore. And remember, no whining, "What are we? I need to know!" A simple "Hey, just to be clear, we are dating?" will suffice. Oh, damn! Look at you now!

6. THOU SHALT DO THY THANG.

Raise your right hand and repeat: "On my honor, I will never again make someone else the center of my world." Good—now live by this. This means: go ahead, date, be in a real relationship, hell, even get married, but always hold on to who you are, because that's what draws people to you. It's one thing to strut your stuff while you're single, but for you, once you're in a relationship, you're going to have the urge to drop everything and hold on to your lover for dear life. Being in a relationship is no excuse for bailing on your friends, or for giving up on your book of poetry, or for letting your gym membership expire. No matter what, you have to have a life outside of the person you're dating. No one wants to be the center of someone's world. It's too much work and it gets boring after a while.

You need to keep doing the things you do that made that person fall for you in the first place. You need a passion beyond being their significant other. Whether it's surfing, playing the banjo, rock climbing, or making finger puppets, hold on to your passions for dear life. Remember, your Friend Zone brain is going to tell you differently. Your brain will say, "Hold on to the person you're dating as hard as you can, never leave their side, show them they are everything to you." Now, tell your brain to shut up, because it's wrong, and do exactly the opposite. Have a life outside of the relationship, go out into the world, scrounge up some stories to tell them when you come back home, and do that thing, whatever it is, that makes you happy—and that has nothing to do with anyone else. That's something that's yours and yours alone, and for once, you don't have to share.

7. THOU SHALT WORK THE SEXY.

No more asexual Mr. or Miss Magoo for you. You will flirt and tease and join in when people are talking about sexual things. You will be part of the adults' club.

Let's face it. The fact that you had no sex appeal was what led your friend to believe there was no potential for sleeping with you. As much as you can, remind members of the opposite sex that although you are not a creepy sex fiend, you are in fact someone who likes sexy time just as much as the next person. And every once in a while, check in with your other friends and make sure you aren't presenting yourself as asexual.

8. THOU SHALT NOT BITCH, MOAN, AND COMPLAIN.

Who's got a thundercloud hanging over their head? Not you! You are a little ray of sunshine! Sure, things may not always go your way, but you are not one to spend your life complaining and feeling sorry for yourself. And even if you do, you keep it to yourself. Why? Because Debbie Downer is always the last to get laid. People don't like to be around someone who bitches, moans, and complains all the time. Negativity and self-loathing are just not sexy.

Also, if you constantly put yourself down and complain about your life, those around you might start looking at you negatively too. Most of us are attracted to positive, smiling, shiny happy people. So, if you make it your business to walk the walk, you might actually feel better too, and that will attract more action.

9. THOU SHALT NOT PUT ALL THY EGGS IN ONE BASKET.

Pinning all your hopes and dreams on one person is part of what landed you in the Friend Zone to begin with. No one can possibly live up to you putting everything—including your future children—in their lap. Remember, not only is there more to life, there are more people out there to date. Don't put everything on one person. First of all, they won't like it, and second, you will be disappointed. People are people, not gods. They are imperfect and mess up, so don't make them the center of your universe.

Until you are fully committed, you need to date around. Getting to know other people before zeroing in on one person is what normal people do, and yes, we are striving for normal here. So as much as it will pain you, try not to devote all your fantasies to one face.

10. THOU SHALT NOT SETTLE FOR LESS.

You know now what it feels like to live in the Friend Zone. You know the loneliness, the fear, and the anxiety. And now that you've lived through it, would you ever want to experience that again? No, of course not. So don't. Don't accept anything less than a real relationship ever again. Promise yourself that you won't ever settle for less. By that, we don't mean only dating models for the rest of your life or constantly going for people who are out of your league. What we mean is don't settle for a pseudo-relationship with someone who doesn't value you as an equal partner. Don't settle for someone's sloppy seconds or leftover cheesecake. Never feel satisfied until you've gotten the real thing, which is someone who loves you, values you, and realizes how amazing you are.

LAST WORDS

Staying out of the Friend Zone means retaining the power in the beginning of the relationship and realizing your self-worth. It's about breaking the unhealthy pattern of clinging to the person you like and instead letting go and trusting that they will realize on their own how amazing you are. It's about trusting that the best way to have a good relationship is not by forcing it or tricking someone into liking you by being their BFF; instead, focus on your own life and have faith that the person you are supposed to be with will see on their own what you have to offer. It's about refraining from devoting your life to someone who isn't your significant other, but rather having them earn that place in your life by entering into a relationship with you. Don't be that person—the one who always sits on the sidelines while other people fall in love. That was you before you read this book, but not now, or ever again.

Your new mantra will forever be: "I'm not giving it away for free. This belongs only to the person who wants me and wants to be with me in a real, honest, 'Mom, Dad, this is my girlfriend or boyfriend' kind of way. Not a 'Mom, Dad, this is my friend, or whatever they are ummm . . . er . . . never mind' kind of way."

And yes, you've changed, and changing is uncomfortable. But now that you've seen the light, going back is going to be even more awkward than moving forward. You are not the person you were when you began this journey. You started in the little hole that was the Friend Zone, you wormed your way out, and now you will stop at nothing to stay above ground. Now you know that your love and your time are valuable, that you will not settle for less, that you don't need to smother someone to get their attention, that being someone's shoulder to cry on will not win their affection, and last but not least, that you are worthy of love—not for what you do, but for who you are.

❖❖❖❖❖❖❖

Joey: It's never gonna happen.

Ross: What?

Joey: You and Rachel.

Ross: Why not?

Joey: You waited too long to make your move, and now you're in the Friend Zone.

Ross: No, no, no. I'm not in the zone.

Joey: Ross, you're the mayor of the zone.

—Friends

❖❖❖❖❖❖❖

Index

❖ ❖ ❖

❖ ❖ ❖

W

❖ ❖ ❖

Y